Discovering Mount St. Helens

Discovering

A Guide to the

Seattle and London

Mount St. Helens

National Volcanic Monument

Scott Shane

UNIVERSITY OF WASHINGTON PRESS

For my mother

Library of Congress Cataloging in Publication Data
Shane, Scott, 1950–
  Discovering Mount St. Helens.
  Bibliography: p.
  Includes index.
  1. Mount Saint Helens National Volcanic Monument (Wash.)
—Guide-books. I. Title.
F897.S17S52 1985   917.97'84   84-40662
ISBN 0-295-96222-4

Title page photo: *Mount St. Helens and Spirit Lake Basin from Mount Margaret*

Contents

Preface

The eruption of Mount St. Helens changed not only the surrounding landscape but the lives of thousands of people living in the Pacific Northwest. One such life was mine. When I heard that the mountain had erupted, my initial feeling was one of loss, as if an old friend had gone. In my mind were images of what had been: a snow-capped peak towering over the landscape, graceful in form, gentle in character. Spirit Lake was deep green, encased by slopes cloaked with old-growth timber. The Mount Margaret backcountry represented a haven in which solitude and peace of mind could be found.

With the commencement of volcanic activity, my weekends were spent around the volcano, photographing its many moods. The only weekend spent away from the mountain was when it chose to erupt. Had the eruption occurred one week earlier, I might not have been alive to tell this story.

Today, my feeling of loss has been replaced by awe and excitement. Working as an interpretive naturalist at the National Volcanic Monument, I have witnessed a landscape in transition. A terrain of varied shades of gray is again becoming green, supporting numerous species of vegetation. The eerie silence of the devastated area has been broken by the songs of birds and the presence of deer and elk. The rapid recovery of life is a reminder that the eruption was not a unique event, but only one incident in a dynamic process. Mount St. Helens has erupted numerous times in the past and will, in all probability, erupt in the future.

This book tells a story of birth and rebirth, the past, present, and possible future of Mount St. Helens. To acknowledge the many persons who made this book possible, pages would be needed. I would like to extend to all of those involved my deepest gratitude. And to Mount St. Helens, a continued close relationship.

The development of a guidebook about Mount St. Helens required information from many academic disciplines. The author would like to express his appreciation to the following persons for time, energy, and assistance in reviewing the manuscript for scientific and historical accuracy: Dr. Grant W. Sharpe, Dr. Fiorenzo C. Ugolini, and Professor Gordon A. Bradley in the College of Forest Resources, University of Washington, for their advice during preparation and critical review of the manuscript. Dr. Chris Newhall, Dr. Donald Peterson, Lyn Topinka, Steve Brantley, and Harry Glicken in the U.S. Geological Survey, and Dr. Anthony J. Irving and Dr. Darrel S. Cowan in the Department of Geological Sciences, University of Washington, for the many hours spent reviewing sections of this text. Dr. Alfred Runte in the Department of History, University of Washington, and Barbara Hollenbeck, archaeologist and historian for the Gifford Pinchot National Forest, for editorial comments on the cultural history chapter. Dr. Kenneth J. Raedeke in the College of Forest Resources, Dr. John S. Edwards in the Department of Zoology, University of Washington, Dr. James MacMahon, Utah State University, Lyle Burmeister, fisheries biologist for Gifford Pinchot National Forest, and Alice Purcell and Frank Roberts, wildlife biologists for the National Volcanic Monument, for assistance on the wildlife chapter. Dr. Thomas M. Hinckley in the College of Forest Resources, Dr. Roger Del Moral in the Department of Botany, University of Washington, and John Gamon, plant biologist for the Malheur National Forest, for time devoted to the vegetation chapter. Jim Neiland, visitor information specialist for the National Volcanic Monument, Wayne Parsons, assistant recreation staff officer for the Gifford Pinchot National Forest, James Quiring, assistant director of the National Volcanic Monument Visitor Center, John Kadow, trail foreman, James Gale, naturalist supervisor, and David Ek, interpretive naturalist, for comments concerning interpretive site and trail description. Grateful appreciation is also given to Chang Chi-Tsen (Paul) for the long hours he so kindly devoted to the development of illustrations. My most significant helper was Rebecca W. Andrews-Shane, who offered her constructive criticism and thorough editing of the book.

Finally, most thanks are due Kathleen Leona Arnold, my mother, whose support and understanding gave me the strength to change course in life and pursue a dream. In her loving memory this book is dedicated.

SCOTT SHANE

Discovering Mount St. Helens

Eruption!

The Mountain Roars: 1980

On March 20, 1980, a series of earthquakes, registering as high as 4.1 on the Richter scale, shook Mount St. Helens. University of Washington seismologists issued an alert indicating the possibility of an eruption. By March 25 earthquakes were shaking the mountain almost continually, increasing the concern of scientists and various governmental authorities.

Based on types and amounts of volcanic debris found at Mount St. Helens, in 1978 Dwight Crandell and Donal Mullineaux of the U.S. Geological Survey forecast that Mount St. Helens could erupt before the end of the century.

The 123-year dormancy (1857–1980) ended on March 27 at 12:30 P.M. when an explosion just beneath the summit sent plumes of steam and ash high into the air and formed a crater in the summit's thick glacial ice cap. Concerned by the significant increase in seismicity, the U.S. Geological Survey issued a formal "hazard watch" statement to state and federal agencies. On March 29 a second crater was observed. Both craters enlarged as eruptions continued, so that by April 7 they merged into one, more than 1,700 feet across and 500 feet deep. On April 3, harmonic tremor was recorded by University of Washington seismologists, prompting the governor of Washington to declare a state of emergency. Harmonic tremor is a type of seismic signal that scientists associate with the underground movement of magma or gases.

From mid-April to May 17, eruptive activity diminished, but seismic energy release remained high. In early April, scientists, comparing aerial photographs taken before and after the beginning of eruptive activity, noticed the growth of a bulge on the upper north slopes of Mount St. Helens. The north flank of the volcano was expanded outward by more than 300 feet and was growing northward at an average rate of 5 to 6 feet per day. It was thought that the bulge was caused by an intrusion of magma into the volcano. Scientists expressed concern that the distended area on the north side of the mountain was weak and might avalanche.

Plinian column rising from Mount St. Helens, May 1980

Beginning eruption activity, March 1980 (looking south, with Dog's Head near left ridge line and Goat Rocks slightly right of center)

The morning of May 18 was crystal clear, offering scientists and volcano watchers an unobstructed view of the volcano. The activity during these early morning hours was much as it had been for the preceding month. No eruptions had been observed for four days, and seismicity, although high, was no greater than it had been for many weeks. The bulge, which now appeared as a large protuberance on the north side of the mountain, continued to deform at a uniform rate.

Phase 1: Debris Avalanche

Suddenly, at 8:32 A.M. PDT, a magnitude-5.1 earthquake triggered the collapse of the mountain's bulging north flank. Propelled by gravity, more than 0.65 cubic mile of rock, snow, and ice avalanched from the volcano's north flank at speeds greater than 200 mph.

One part plunged into Spirit Lake, raising the lake's surface level by roughly 200 feet. Huge waves formed which surged up surrounding ridges, leaving wash marks as high as 850 feet above the original lake level. As the water returned to Spirit Lake, it carried with it blown-down timber, which floated on the lake's surface. The surface area of Spirit Lake increased from 1,300 to 2,500 acres, and the outlet for the North Fork Toutle River was blocked

Bulge swelling on upper north flanks, May 17, 1980. Ice avalanches formed dark paths down the northern slopes, originating from the shattered, swelling Forsyth Glacier. Snow-covered Timberline parking lot is at lower right

by a mile-wide barrier of avalanche debris. On May 19, 1980, one day after the eruption, the surface temperature of the lake had soared to 91 degrees F.

Five miles north of the volcano, a 985–1,250-foot-high ridge (now named Johnston Ridge after David A. Johnston, a member of the U.S. Geological Survey who lost his life during the eruption) lay in the path of the avalanche. Debris moved over the ridge and into South Coldwater Creek drainage on the opposite side. But the bulk of the debris avalanche was deflected by the ridge and swept down the North Fork Toutle River. In only 10 minutes the debris flowed 13.5 miles and covered over 24 square miles of the river valley to an average depth of 150 feet. It consisted of intermixed volcanic debris of various sizes, including boulders, pebbles, sand, silt, and blocks of glacial ice as large as 40 feet across. The thickest part of the deposit, over 640 feet deep, lay 1.5 miles west of Spirit Lake Lodge, managed by Harry Truman.

The effects of the landslide on Mount St. Helens were tremendous. The landslide was the major force that sculptured the crater. The crater sides are steep walled, forming a horseshoe-shaped "amphitheater" open to the north. The rear wall of the amphitheater has a precipitous drop of 2,000 feet from the rim to the crater floor. The crater rim is now 1,313 feet lower than the original summit.

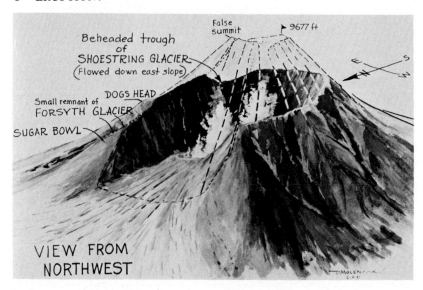

Beheaded trough
of
SHOESTRING GLACIER
(Flowed down east slope)

DOGS HEAD

Small remnant of
FORSYTH GLACIER

SUGAR BOWL

False summit

9677 ft

VIEW FROM
NORTHWEST

Portion of mountain removed (dashed line) May 18, 1980

Phase 2: The Lateral Blast

The loss of the north flank of the volcano released the pressure on the hydrothermal system below, resulting in a huge lateral blast directed across the land. As the debris avalanche raced down the lower flanks of Mount St. Helens, the initial stage of the lateral explosion overtook the avalanche and spread northward at tremendous speeds. David Johnston was alone at the Coldwater II observation station, 5.7 miles from the summit. Watching the debris avalanche and lateral blast cloud race toward him, he attempted to call his headquarters on his radio: "Vancouver, Vancouver, this is it!" The rest of his transmission was too garbled to understand—then silence. A more detailed account of the first seconds of the eruption was radioed by Gerald Martin, a volunteer volcano watcher for the Washington Department of Emergency Services. Positioned on a ridge top 7 miles north of the volcano, he calmly described the unbelievable scene unfolding before him: "The camper and the car just over to the south of me [David Johnston] are covered. . . . It [the lateral blast cloud] is going to get me, too." Seconds later, the cloud swept Gerald Martin to his death. The lateral blast continued about 5 minutes. Pulverized pieces of mountain, hot gases, and organic material contained in the blast cloud moved across the landscape at speeds up to 250

View from Coldwater II observation station, May 17, 1980

View fro... ...mber 20, 1980

The lateral blast transformed stands of forest into complicated patterns of downed and standing dead timber

mph and 680 degrees F., devastating the terrain. Spanning an arc of nearly 180 degrees, the blast affected an area of more than 215 square miles extending 23 miles east to west and as far as 18 miles north from the volcano. Almost all vegetation and wildlife were exterminated within a zone 6 miles north of the mountain. From 6 to 23 miles north of the mountain, the force of the blast was so strong that forests of 200-foot Douglas-fir were blown down or singed. In many places the blast was guided by ridges to form complicated swirl and crisscross patterns of downed and standing dead timber.

A sound wave shot straight up from the volcano and ricocheted back to earth off a hot layer (1500 degrees F.) in the ionosphere nearly 300 miles in altitude. Deflected at various angles, sounds like heavy artillery fire and booms were heard as far as British Columbia, Montana, and California. Yet near the mountain, local populations never heard the blast because the sound was quickly absorbed by the local topography.

Phase 3: Plinian Eruption Column

The term Plinian is taken from the famous Roman naturalist Pliny the Elder, who died while observing the eruption of Vesuvius in A.D. 79. The term is applied to the phase of the eruption during which gas is released upward, forming an eruption cloud.

In fewer than 15 minutes a huge cauliflower-shaped ash column had risen to a height of over 15 miles into the stratosphere (80,000 feet). The eruption continued vigorously for 9 hours, and the prevailing upper winds carried the

Plinian column, May 18, 1980. The white cloud rising through the low layer of airborne ash in the background was caused by steam explosions in hot avalanche deposits near the southwestern end of Spirit Lake

dense clouds of ash in an east-northeast direction, turning daytime into total darkness for more than 125 linear miles.

Flashes of lightning associated with the eruption column started hundreds of fires. Ash was reported in Montana and as far east as the Great Plains, a distance of over 900 miles. Dissipating in the atmosphere, the ash plume passed over New England and across the North Atlantic Ocean. By early June, the ash plume had circumnavigated the globe and returned over the West Coast of North America.

The air-fall ash deposited during the first 9 hours of the eruption amounted to about 540 million tons distributed over an area of more than 22,000 square miles. The volume of uncompacted ash was equal to about 0.05 cubic mile of solid rock, or only about 10 percent of the amount of material that slid off the volcano during the debris avalanche.

Morton, Washington, at 12:28 P.M., May 18, 1980

In ash-blanketed areas of eastern Washington, thousands of motorists were stranded because of poor visibility or stalled cars. The Washington State Department of Transportation reported that 1,100 miles of state roads were closed because of the ash. The fine ash, swirled into clouds by gusts of wind or passing vehicles, worked its way inside homes and automobiles. The ash drifted like snow, but unfortunately did not melt. When mixed with water it assumed the consistency of wet cement. Cleanup was nearly impossible.

Phase 4: Lahars (Mudflows)

Lahar is an Indonesian term used to describe a dense flow of gravel, sand, mud, and water that forms during a volcanic eruption or originates on the slopes of a volcano. These mixtures typically contain 60 percent sediment and 40 percent water by volume. There were two distinct types of lahars produced by Mount St. Helens during the May 18 eruption.

1. During the first minutes of the eruption, the heat and turbulence of the lateral blast and related pyroclastic surges caused rapid melting of snow and

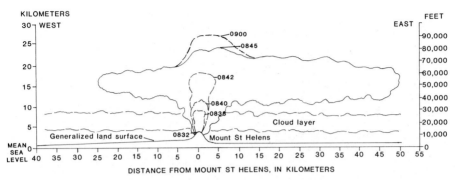

Growth of Plinian eruption column, May 18, 1980. Source: Sarna-Wojciciki et al.

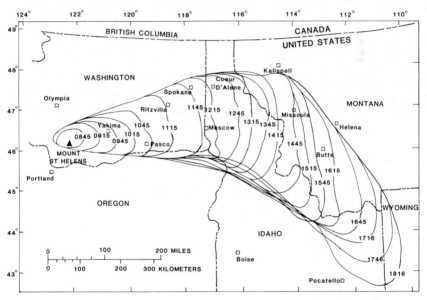

Downwind distribution of ash, May 18, 1980. Source: Sarna-Wojciciki et al.

ice. As these surges rushed down the mountain's flanks, traveling up to 80 mph, they began to decrease in speed, transforming into denser, water-mobilized lahars on the lower slopes of the volcano. Smith Creek, Pine Creek, Muddy River, and the South Fork Toutle River were affected by lahars of this type.

2. Lahars of the North Fork Toutle River formed on the water-saturated debris avalanche deposit. As the deposit settled and compacted, excess water

Bridge and road removed by Muddy River lahar

was forced to its surface and began to flow slowly across the debris avalanche deposit and beyond.

Within minutes of the initial eruption, pyroclastic surges related to the blast
melted snow and ice near the summit. Lahars heavily laden with logs and
forest debris rushed down Smith Creek and Muddy River on the east side of
the mountain, and Pine Creek on the southeastern side. Walls of surging mud
and water as high as 25 feet destroyed sixteen bridges and 12.5 miles of
Forest Service roads. By about 9:20 A.M. the combined Muddy River and

Pine Creek lahars began pouring nearly 500 million cubic feet of debris into the 8.7-mile-long Swift Reservoir, raising its water level by 2.6 feet.

By 10:10 A.M. a lahar on the South Fork Toutle River was 27 miles downstream, where it destroyed Camp 12 logging camp. Trees, buildings, automobiles, and miles of roads were swept away. A deputy near the confluence of the North and South Fork Toutle rivers radioed at 10:14 A.M. that a 12-foot wall of water containing logs, debris, and buildings was swiftly working its way down the river.

The North Fork Toutle River lahar formed in a different way. Between 12:00 and 1:00 P.M., water began to accumulate at the surface of the debris avalanche as the deposit settled. Additional water was supplied by the North Fork Toutle River, now buried, and by melting blocks of glacial ice crumbled by the blast and avalanche. Many small lahars began to form on the surface of the debris avalanche, and by 1:30 P.M. these had coalesced into one huge lahar, which passed beyond the far end of the debris avalanche and moved slowly down the North Fork Toutle River, destroying logging camps, bridges, homes, and other objects in its path. The North Fork Toutle River lahar poured into the Cowlitz River 45 miles away, raising the river's temperature to 90 degrees F. By the following day, about 45 million cubic yards of volcanic sediment had blocked the deepwater navigation channel of the Columbia River 75 miles away, decreasing its channel depth from 40 to 15 feet for a distance of 2 miles.

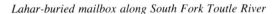

Lahar-buried mailbox along South Fork Toutle River

Phase 5: Pyroclastic Flows

The term "pyroclastic" is derived from the Greek words *pyro* (fire) and *klastos* (broken). It describes materials formed by the fragmentation of magma and rock by explosive volcanic activity. A pyroclastic flow is a lateral flowage of a turbulent mixture of hot gases, entrapped air, and unsorted pyroclastic volcanic material (ash, pumice, and dense rock) that can move at speeds in excess of 100 mph. There are two major parts to a pyroclastic flow: a ground-hugging basal flow composed of the unsorted material, and a cloud of gases and fine-grained dust riding above the basal flow, called the surge.

At 12:17 P.M. a USGS geologist monitoring the eruption noticed a rapid change in the color of the Plinian eruption column—from a medium gray to dirty white. The color change was attributed to greater amounts of new rock—and less old rock—being ejected from chambers deep beneath the volcano. The color change is believed to have signaled a shift to a nearly pure magmatic eruption of fresh pumice. Pyroclastic flows occurred during this magmatic phase of the ongoing Plinian eruption.

Not all the ejecta rose high enough or were light enough to be carried east by the wind. Some of the pumice blocks and ash flowed north out of the breached crater and formed a fanlike pattern of overlapping sheets, tongues,

Pyroclastic flow (formed October 17, 1980) on the pumice plain (Spirit Lake and the Mount Margaret area in the background)

and lobes as far as 5 miles into Spirit Lake and onto parts of the debris avalanche. Temperature measurements taken in these pyroclastic flows still
registered 780 degrees F. two weeks after the eruption. Huge steam plumes
shot into the air as hot rock material met cooler lake water. Phreatic explosion pits, some as large as 300 feet in diameter and 65 feet deep, were formed
when hot pyroclastic flows covered water in streams, ponds, and springs. As
the water flashed to steam, the upward-directed steam explosions reamed holes
in the overlying deposits. These steam explosions continued intermittently
for several months after the flows were deposited. The lateral spreading of
flows was halted by Johnston Ridge, which caused pooling in both the valley of the North Fork Toutle River and Spirit Lake Basin. Much of the irregular topography left by the debris avalanche on the south end of Spirit
Lake was transformed into a huge pumice plain. Mounds of avalanche debris protrude through the pyroclastic flow deposits on the pumice plain. An
area of over 6 square miles was covered to depths of as much as 125 feet.

Even after the ground-hugging basal flows lost momentum, overriding ash
clouds continued traveling over the landscape. Undeterred by topographical
features, ash clouds covered sections of Johnston Ridge and the debris avalanche with dunes of fine grained powdery ash.

Fumaroles or steam columns can be seen rising lazily from the pumice
plain as cooling deposits vent air, steam, and other gases. As the pyroclastic
flow deposits continue to cool, the fumaroles will decrease in size and eventually disappear.

Fumaroles rising from pumice plain

Subsequent Eruptive Activity

Subsequent explosive eruptions of Mount St. Helens occurred on May 25, June 12, July 22, August 7, and October 16–18, 1980, and March 19, 1982. These eruptions were not as large as those of May 18, but each eruption produced spectacular ash columns 25,000 to 50,000 feet above sea level and boiling pyroclastic flows which swept down the north flank of the volcano. Following the eruption of June 12, a small lava dome grew within the crater to a size of about 1,200 feet in diameter and 140 feet high. This dome was largely destroyed by the July 22 eruption. A new dome grew after the August 7 eruption but was mostly removed on October 16. A new dome began to grow in the crater on October 19, 1980, and survived to form the core of the present dome. As of November 1984, about 15 dome-building events, predominantly nonexplosive, have increased the size of the dome. Eruptions of 1981–82 were episodic, occurring every one to five months. This pattern changed between February 1983 and February 1984, when the dome grew continuously as magma was pumped into it, causing it to swell from within. As the dome expanded, numerous pressure cracks formed on its surface from which thick lava oozed. As the lava crept down its sides, it cooled and hardened, increasing the size of the rugged, bread-crust textured dome to roughly 810 feet in height and 2,800 feet in diameter. As of May 1984, Mount St. Helens appears to have returned to the episodic pattern of dome growth, with dome-building events occurring in March, June, July, and September. Scientists estimate that if the dome continues to grow at its present rate, it will take about 150 to 200 years for the volcano to regain its preeruption form.

As of
Aug. 1988
Dome
3000 ft x 1500 ft high

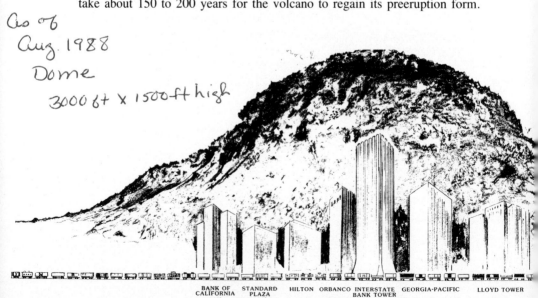

| BANK OF CALIFORNIA 268' | STANDARD PLAZA 233' | HILTON 249' | ORBANCO 364' | INTERSTATE BANK TOWER 536' | GEORGIA-PACIFIC 375' | LLOYD TOWER 290' |

Scientists working (lower left corner) on dome's rubbly surface

Of course, it is possible that the dome will cease to grow or will be blown away by another eruption and the process of dome building started again.

Today, visitors to the monument frequently view white steam plumes, or blue tinted plumes if mixed with gas, rising from the dome within the crater. Less frequently, dark plumes filled with gas and ash thrill onlookers. Extensive monitoring is enabling scientists to predict more accurately the type and timing of eruptions at Mount St. Helens, forecasting eruptive events hours or even days before they occur. As this understanding improves, more of the monument's affected areas will be opened to the general public.

In the final analysis, all actions depend on the behavior of the volcano itself. Most likely, Mount St. Helens will continue its present dome building, with or without occasional explosive activity, and then become quiet once more.

Lava dome compared to the city center of Portland, Oregon

52 RAILROAD BOXCARS LONG

Life Erased—Life Renewed

The destruction of vegetation and wildlife during the devastating eruptions of 1980 was not a unique occurrence, but only one brief battle in the cyclic nature of earth and life forces. For Mount St. Helens the struggle started a mere 40,000 years ago with the birth of the volcano.

Evidence of old battles is everywhere. On the north slope of the volcano, the timberline had been lowered repeatedly by the onslaught of erupted pyroclastic material, most recently in the first half of the nineteenth century. In an attempt to regain their ecological niche, tree species that had been established at 4,200 feet were progressing up to the climatic limit of 6,500 feet above sea level, where a timberline is normally established in the Cascade Range at that latitude. On the south slopes, forests of lodgepole pine occupy areas which were affected by pyroclastic and lahar activity only 350 to 450 years ago. These stands are adjacent to older, unaffected land forms where the fertile soils support noble fir and Douglas-fir.

Battle scars can also be seen in the records of tree rings. To the northeast of the mountain, the effects of historic eruptions in A.D. 1480 and 1800 can be seen in the annual rings of trees that survived these events. Many trees failed to put on growth for several years following these eruptions.

Plants and animals that survived the eruption of May 18, 1980, and those now recolonizing the devastated area from outside provide the basis for re-establishment of plant and animal communities. The successional process is not one overall process that is occurring throughout the area but a mosaic of processes, each contingent on a certain set of circumstances.

Tephra rained from the sky on May 18, blanketing trees outside the blast area with a thick coating of ash

19

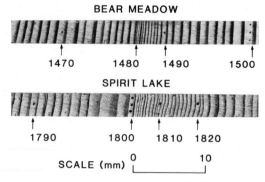

Narrow-ring patterns in Douglas-fir date eruptions of tephra layers Wn (white-north) and T (Timberline) to A.D. *1480 (Bear Meadow) and 1800 (Spirit Lake)*

Plants

Preeruption

Preeruption vegetation had evolved over many centuries following previous devastation and had come to match that elsewhere in western Washington. Spirit Lake appeared as a jewel cast in a setting of deep green. Huge old-growth Douglas-fir, western red cedar, western hemlock, western white pine, and noble fir ascended steep walls rising nearly 2,000 feet above the lake. As red and Sitka alder, vine and Rocky Mountain maple, and black cotton-wood turned color during autumn, splashes of orange, red, and yellow were added to the landscape.

Under the dense, lush canopy of the forest was a diverse understory of plant species. Numerous trails led to waist-high patches of red and oval-leaf huckleberry, where hours could be spent picking and devouring the succulent fruits. In autumn, leaves from these species turned a brilliant red. Currant, salal, and sword fern also carpeted the forest floor.

Trails led to the Mount Margaret backcountry and Mount St. Helens proper. In a landscape dotted by multiple small lakes in a rugged setting of cliffs and subalpine vegetation, sturdy stands of Pacific silver fir, subalpine fir, lodgepole pine, and mountain hemlock prospered, defying the harsh environment. Slopes covered by subalpine meadows rose sharply from crystal clear lakes. Wind and snow swept ridge lines were cloaked in mountain heath, juniper, salal, and countless species of perennial wildflowers, adding to the breathtaking panorama of Spirit Lake and Mount St. Helens.

Mount St. Helens and Spirit Lake Basin as they appeared from the Mount Margaret backcountry before the 1980 eruption

Posteruption

The May 18 eruption of Mount St. Helens resulted in widespread destruction of vegetation in the path of the lateral blast on the north side of the volcano. Vegetation on the south side was relatively untouched, affected only slightly by lahars and tephra fallout. In an 180-degree arc extending as far as 19 miles northward from the volcano, over 150,000 acres of forest and recreation lands were devastated. The most severe vegetative losses occurred in the Spirit Lake Basin and Mount Margaret area, where the full impact of the blast was directed. (The entire mountain goat population residing on the steep ridges of the Mount Margaret area was exterminated.) With the collapse of the north side of the mountain, the huge debris avalanche smothered forests and plants under hundreds of feet of highly erodible, nutrient-poor debris.

Pyroclastic flows that surged out of the mouth of the yawning crater also buried forests under boiling material. The released lateral blast either vaporized forests or covered blown-down remnants with varying depths of hot ash and lapilli. Even on the outer fringes of the blast zone vegetation was not spared. Over 19 miles north of the crater, hot air scorched forests, killing trees. Raging lahars extended the vegetative damage as trees and plants along distant riverbanks were swept away. The few trees that managed to remain upright were doomed to root suffocation from restricted air flow due to soil compaction.

Views from summit of Mount Margaret (8.5 miles north-northeast of Mount St. Helens) before the May 18 eruption and after

This view of Goat Mountain, with Ryan Lake in the right foreground, shows the fine line between life and death

Covering an even greater area was a zone of air-fall tephra. The huge eruption cloud deposited material on forests as far away as Montana. The most spectacular deposits were found along a transect from Elk Pass to Chambers Lake, located 11 and 35 miles respectively to the northeast of the volcano. In this region, tephra rained from the sky almost the entire day of May 18. The forests appeared to be covered by gray snow. This covering persisted relatively unchanged until the first storms in the fall. It reduced growth of the total tree in several ways. Photosynthesis was hampered when light could not reach encased needles. The tephra coating, when baked by the summer sun, often reached temperatures near 120 degrees F., burning the needles.

Almost immediately after the initial eruption, a massive rescue effort was undertaken by federal, state, and military authorities to search for survivors. Rescuers entered a destroyed world where cars and campers were tumbled about like toys, buildings and homes had been crumpled, and roads were obliterated. In all directions, the landscape appeared void of life. Spirit Lake could not be located and was thought to have been removed by the debris avalanche and blast. Forests that had graced the rugged slopes were non-existent. It seemed that total annihilation had occurred.

Upper Muddy lahar, 1980

Deeply eroded upper Muddy lahar, 1981

changing from gray to green. Small pockets of purple-flowered thistle, arrowleaf grounsel, fireweed, pearly everlasting, and lupine are just a few of the plant species that add life and color to the landscape.

Although it was buried under varying depths of tephra, the soil played a significant role in ensuring successful recovery of vegetation, for it contained nutrients and communities of microorganisms that supplied essential ingredients for plant survival. In contrast, the hot tephra deposited over hundreds of square miles was void of most nutrients needed for healthy plant growth. Nitrogen and phosphorus, two essential nutrients, were nearly nonexistent. The few nutrients that were contained in the tephra were quickly leached out by rain water.

The buried soil contained numerous kinds of fungi, which formed close symbiotic associations (called mycorrhizae) with plant roots. Fungi grow on, between, and within cells of plant roots, increasing the surface area available to the plant for water and nutrient uptake. A single cubic millimeter of soil can contain as much as 13 feet of hyphae, threadlike extensions that make up the fungal mycelia. Fungi help plants withstand drought and nutrient-deficient soils, especially where nitrogen and phosphorus are lacking. In this symbiotic relationship, the fungi receive food from the host in return for supplying the plant with nutrients and water.

Fireweed

Pearly everlasting

Pacific lupine

One way fungi are dispersed through the soil strata is by the burrowing habits of pocket gophers. With the deposition of nutrient-poor tephra, recolonizing plants had little chance of contacting fungi contained in the buried soil. Pocket gophers serve as a tiller, bringing nutrient-rich soil containing fungi to the tephra layer. Plants soon established themselves on pocket gopher mound material as opposed to adjacent nongopher material. These islands of vegetation acted as bases of life from which plants spread to surrounding areas.

Over four-fifths of the earth's atmosphere is made up of gaseous nitrogen. Most plants are not capable of transforming this nitrogen into chemical compounds essential for their existence. But a few plants such as lupine and red alder can perform this function. Bacterial organisms concentrated in nodules on their root tissue are capable of chemically converting atmospheric nitrogen into forms usable by their host plant. The bacteria incorporate nitrogen into compounds of nitrates and ammonia, which are then used by the host plant. Lupine, alder, and other species involved in symbiotic relationships with nitrogen-fixing bacteria are successfully reestablishing themselves throughout the devastated area.

In those areas devoid of plant life, the plants with nitrogen-fixing abilities (lupines, alder, vetches, etc.) are the first to invade. Over time these will decay, providing nitrogen for plants that cannot fix atmospheric nitrogen, and so continue the cycle of life.

Plant communities on the south flank of Mount St. Helens represent what much of the area on the north side looked like before the 1980 eruptions. One can sense the beauty and grandeur that once graced the shores of Spirit Lake and the ridge lines of the Mount Margaret backcountry. A closer look shows that forest communities on the volcano's southern slopes are in varying stages of revegetation, depending on when they were last affected by volcanic activity.

One such area is the Cave Basalt region, indicative of the terrain surrounding Ape Cave and Lava Casts, where pioneer plant communities are taking hold in a rugged volcanic environment. The lava flow substrate, generated about 1,900 years ago, is composed of a dry, rocky soil, low in nutrients. The lower-elevation forest community is dominated by lodgepole pine, with small components of Douglas-fir, subalpine fir, and western white pine. The low fertility of the soil allows only the heartiest understory plants to survive, of which bearberry and Oregon boxwood are the most prevalent. The forest floor is covered with multiple shades of green generated by a wide variety of mosses and lichens thriving on the rocky soil.

On the southern slopes of the volcano, timberline occurs near 4,400 feet. It has been kept low by periodic eruptions. As a result, the forest community is quite diverse, consisting of moderate- and high-elevation tree species within a narrow elevation range. Trees that normally live at higher elevations continue to move up the slopes, gradually filling the habitat available to them.

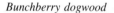

Bunchberry dogwood

Aerial view of Goat Marsh

The short growing season requires that plant species be well adapted to cold temperatures and low soil moisture and nutrient levels. Subalpine fir dominates the overstory, with fewer numbers of lodgepole pine, western white pine, and mountain hemlock. The understory is limited mainly to mountain huckleberry, bear grass, and some parsley fern. Mosses and lichens contribute the greatest variety of understory cover.

In the lush environment of the Goat Marsh area one finds a wide variety of ecosystems within a relatively small area. Open water, marsh, and swamp wetlands are occupied by plant communities of sedges and grasses, willows, and blueberries, each well adapted to surviving in saturated organic soils.

Adjacent to the wetlands, old-growth noble fir, towering over 270 feet with a diameter of 7 feet, occupy the lower mountain slopes and flats. Adding to the overstory, Douglas-fir, Pacific silver fir, and western hemlock seem to pierce the sky. Under this dense old-growth canopy, vine maple, oak fern, and deerfoot vanilla leaf complement the diverse understory.

Rising from the Goat Marsh area, steep, broken terrain is covered by a Pacific silver fir and western hemlock forest. The steep forest floor is matted with wildflowers such as coolwort foamflower, false lily of the valley, and prince's pine, to name a few.

A lodgepole pine forest exists on the deposits of the Kalama River lahar in the vicinity of the Goat Marsh area. Lodgepole pine dominates the overstory, while bearberries, lichens, and mosses cover the forest floor. Along the banks of streams that have cut through the deposit, a rich variety of flora partly consisting of sitka alder, alpine willoweed, and common monkeyflower add a lining of color.

North of the lahar forest, the overstory becomes dominated by black cottonwood, red alder, and minor components of noble fir and western hemlock. A diverse understory of vine maple, queencup (beadlily), bunchberry dogwood, false lily of the valley, coolwort foamflower, and pioneer violet are a few of the plant species that can be seen.

Avalanche lily   *Columbine*   *Columbia lily*

Animals

Terrestrial Wildlife

Before the eruption of Mount St. Helens, hundreds of species of birds, mammals, and other wildlife thrived within the boundaries of the monument. On the morning of May 18, survival of wildlife depended primarily on their location and distance from the volcano. The majority of animals in the path of the blast were exterminated. Hurricane force winds filled with volcanic and organic debris, superheated to hundreds of degrees, swept most animals to their death.

Despite this bleak epitaph, there were many survivors. An unusual set of circumstances often determined whether an organism would live or die. Larger terrestrial mammals that lived year-round above ground had little chance to escape the fury of the blast. Smaller mammals, however, were often underground in burrows at the time of the eruption. Remarkably, all the species of small mammals that existed in the devastated area before the eruption were found alive in protected islands of survival surrounded by a sea of destruction. One of the most amazing stories of survival has to do with the Spirit Lake Basin, the area most affected by the eruption. On the morning of May 18, pocket gophers were hibernating in their underground burrows on ridges surrounding Spirit Lake. These ridges were hit full force by the lateral blast, and waves from Spirit Lake, generated by the impact of the debris avalanche, scoured ridge slopes to bedrock. Although the vast majority of pocket gophers were killed, in isolated spots land forms such as rock outcrops deflected the lateral blast, causing it to pass harmlessly overhead, leaving pocket gopher communities virtually untouched. By August 1980, numerous pocket gopher communities were found dotting the blasted ridges, some within a few feet of the scour line above Spirit Lake. Chipmunks, weasels, deer mice, and other small animal species also took part in this scenario of survival.

Numerous species of insects and spiders also survived the eruption and are successfully multiplying. Protected at the moment of the blast in the bark of trees or in underground nests were ground beetles, spiders, harvestmen, centipedes, millipedes, and camel crickets, among others. Those insects that were predators, scavengers, or fungi eaters were able to find food and proved best able to adapt to the newly created volcanic environment.

Within weeks of the eruption, ants were observed on top of blast deposits. The ants remained underground in their nests and waited until the hot tephra deposits cooled, at which time they burrowed to the surface. They were able to survive the short term by feeding on other insects that were dying or dead

Elk browsing on seeded portion of debris avalanche (near North Fork Toutle River)

and from colony food reserves. After vegetation began to reappear, additional food sources became available. As aphids colonized the new vegetation, ants were able to use honeydew from the aphids to provide their energy needs. Nectar from floral or extrafloral nectaries also supplied food.

For many animals, survival through the eruption phase was not enough to ensure their continued existence and habitation of the area. The volcanic environment was in a continual state of flux, forcing survivors to adapt to varied and extreme conditions.

Many animals that survived the blast were not found in the spring of 1981. The widespread destruction of above-ground vegetation had resulted in the elimination of almost all suitable wildlife habitat. In certain areas, pocket gophers, which feed underground on roots, bulbs, corms, and rhizomes, were adversely affected because the available food in their foraging area was soon exhausted or the surviving plants did not supply the nutrients they needed. In this case, populations that had survived the blast soon diminished from starvation. In other areas, however, vegetative islands of survival provided the diversity of plant species necessary to fulfill the nutrient requirements of the pocket gopher. Under these conditions they have survived and are breeding. As of 1984, thirty-five breeding colonies of pocket gophers have been located on the ridges surrounding Spirit Lake alone.

Recolonization of the blast zone is also occurring through the movement of animals from more distant, unaffected areas surrounding the National Volcanic Monument. Invertebrates, such as spiders and winged ground beetles, fly into devastated areas on wind currents. Spiders use a particularly inventive means for making this journey. Many species spin thin threads of silk that remain attached to their spinnerets and act like a balloon. Winds whisk invertebrates into the air, transporting them for miles, landing some involuntarily in the blast zone. The majority soon die from exposure to harsh environmental conditions or to the appetites of waiting carnivorous invertebrates. If by chance, however, they land near an object that supplies protection against the elements, such as a plant, crack, or rock underside, the chance for survival is greater. Today, over forty species of spiders have been found on the pumice plain, as diverse a population as in a city park.

Highly mobile immigrants such as deer, elk, and birds were soon observed in devastated areas. The large mammals often use riparian (stream and lakeside) corridors for access into blast areas. Within weeks of the eruption, deer and elk were sighted on the debris avalanche and areas just north of Spirit Lake. As these animals crisscrossed the tephra-covered landscape they broke up the tephra layer, increasing rilling action. Plants soon took hold in these disturbed areas, turning animal paths into lines of green.

Birds have returned to green edge zones that border singed timberland. Launching daily feeding forays into affected areas, the birds penetrate deep

Common nighthawk in blowdown zone

Killdeer nest on debris avalanche

into the devastated zone, where they have been observed nesting. But birds may not repopulate the devastated zone to their previous numbers. Before the eruption, many of the bird species inhabiting the area were conifer seed eaters or insectivores dependent on an old-growth forest. The blast eliminated food and shelter necessary for their survival. Only if the habitat recovers to its preeruption condition will the needs of many bird species be met. This type of forest will take hundreds of years to return to its original state, and with today's timber needs, this may not happen.

Adequate shelter is also a requirement for bird repopulation. By destroying old-growth stands, the blast eliminated suitable habitat for many birds dependent on late-succession forests, such as the spotted owl, pileated woodpecker, and the black-backed three-toed woodpecker. But new snag habitat was provided by the searing heat which killed standing timber at the edge of the blast zone. This new habitat is capable of supporting an abundance of early successional, snag-dependent bird species by providing internal and external sites for nesting, roosting, resting, and hiding. Hairy woodpeckers, which excavate cavities in snags while searching for insects, were observed in early 1981. Soon to follow were nonexcavator birds, such as mountain bluebirds, tree swallows, and winter wrens, which seek out these cavities for nesting. Birds of prey such as the red-tailed hawk and the sparrow hawk have also been seen foraging and nesting in snag areas.

Aquatic Life

Prior to the eruption, rivers, streams, and lakes that surrounded Mount St. Helens offered some of the finest game fishing in Washington State. Abundant spawning and fish-rearing habitats existed for numerous fish species.

The North Fork Toutle River provided a rich habitat for coho salmon and lesser numbers of chinook salmon. The Muddy and South Fork Toutle were two rivers that contained resident rainbow and brook trout. Swift, Yale, and Merwin reservoirs attracted anglers from around the state hoping to catch a large coho or kokanee. Spirit Lake contained rainbow, brook, and cutthroat trout, in addition to providing spawning beds in its smaller tributaries for coho salmon and trout. Alpine lakes, nestled among the Mount Margaret range, had been planted with cutthroat, rainbow, and brook trout since the beginning of this century.

The cataclysmic eruption of Mount St. Helens had an immediate and profound effect on the majority of lakes, rivers, and streams in the monument, and the aquatic life that they supported. The North Fork Toutle River was inundated by the huge debris avalanche averaging 150 feet in depth, turning the formerly V-shaped canyon into a broad U-shaped one. Little aquatic life was left in the wake of the debris avalanche. High concentrations of ash and mud in the water produced gill abrasion in fish, resulting in suffocation or loss of body fluids. Later in the day, hot pyroclastic flows mixed with the upper portions of the debris avalanche, raising the water temperature of the

St. Helens Lake soon after the May 18 eruption

North Fork Toutle River to nearly 100 degrees for a distance of 20 miles from the crater.

On the southeast side of the volcano, Smith, Ape Canyon, and Pine creeks, and the Muddy River were in the process of being scoured by lahars. Many streams that fed these mainstream systems were scraped to bedrock by debris torrents. Riparian habitat was removed, reducing streams to highly exposed, high-velocity environments unsuitable for spawning and fish rearing.

Aquatic life was heavily affected in lakes, rivers, and streams in the path of the lateral blast. Spawning habitats in these locations suffered greatly when mainstream spawning gravels were choked with ash, mud, and pumice. Reproduction will be considerably reduced until these spawning gravels are flushed of such deposits.

In many streams death was not immediate. Many aquatic vertebrates and invertebrates existing before the eruption were found in the summer of 1980. But heavy rains during the following winter eroded volcanic material from surrounding steep slopes, carrying it into valley bottom streams. So much material entered these tributaries that it scoured stream bottoms. By the spring of 1981, most aquatic life had been killed. Unlike terrestrial plant life, for which erosional processes proved mostly beneficial by exposing buried plant parts, for aquatic organisms it often meant death.

Despite the amount of overall destruction to water systems, repopulation of aquatic organisms is taking place in most monument water bodies. Fish living in less affected smaller tributaries are reproducing and immigrating to mainstream systems. In turn, they are migrating up or down streams into tributaries that were scoured. In Meta Lake, brook trout fry were found in 1983. A sampling of high-country lakes in the Mount Margaret area during 1980–82 indicated that at least 70 percent contained populations of trout that survived the eruption. Their survival is partly attributed to the fact that higher elevation lakes were covered by ice, which served as a protective shield against air-fall pyroclastic material. Natural reproduction of rainbow and cutthroat trout occurred at a low rate in these lakes prior to 1980, because of lack of proper spawning habitat. Their numbers were kept constant through periodic stocking. Fish surviving the eruption are again reproducing at a slow rate in these lakes. It may come to pass that if stocking is not continued, fish populations may slowly dwindle and eventually die off, leaving some of these lakes void of fish, as they were before stocking.

Many lakes within 15 miles of the volcano in a north or northeasterly direction were severely affected by blown-down and seared timber that was thrown into lakes by the initial blast. This organic material decomposed and adversely affected water quality. For those lakes most heavily affected, water quality soon degraded so badly that they looked like black ooze. Today, most lakes have become clearer and support low levels of aquatic life.

Bacterial and algal populations were still predominant in Grizzly Lake, three years after the eruption

A rapid rise in water temperature due to the blast also occurred in many lakes. Spirit Lake had a surface temperature of 91 degrees on May 19, 1980, compared with a typical May surface temperature of 50 degrees F. Elevated water temperatures combined with decomposing organic material to produce a highly enriched ecosystem devoid of dissolved oxygen, which resulted in a bacterial population explosion. By August 1980, biological communities had shifted completely to anaerobic microorganisms, which could live in water without dissolved oxygen. Scientists became concerned for public safety when *Legionella* sp. and *Klebsiella* pneumonia were discovered in the water of lakes in the devastated area. Today this danger has greatly lessened because of inflows of water from rain and snow melt, which have improved the water quality of the lakes.

Aquatic reptiles and amphibians, such as the salamander and tailed frog, survived the eruption. After hibernating under layers of mud on lake bottoms, salamanders made their way to the surface in the late spring of 1980 and reproduced. Every amphibian and reptilian species that resided in lakes before the eruption is present today. Even in Spirit Lake, most radically affected by the blast, salamanders and frogs have migrated from protected tributary streams and are reproducing.

The "natural" recovery of terrestrial and aquatic habitats is under way. By 1981, stream habitats contained early successional, algae-based communities with low densities of aquatic invertebrates. The number of midges and flies increased by 1982, thus providing a link in the food chain by feeding on the algae and serving as a source of food for fish, which had been feeding predominantly off terrestrial insects through 1981.

Riparian vegetation is pushing through tephra layers to form new habitats. This type of habitat plays a critical role in the food chain of fish, supplies protective cover, binds bank soils, and provides shade, which regulates stream temperatures. The revegetation process is slow; many perennial streams still lack streamside vegetation. This absence of adequate vegetation cover has a negative effect on all forms of aquatic life in the monument streams.

As natural revegetation gradually reclaims this barren landscape, terrestrial and aquatic life will follow. In areas outside monument boundaries, artificial means of aiding nature have been implemented to speed up the recovery process. Forests have been replanted, and snag environments are being left to help wildlife reinvade old territories devastated by the blast. Stream banks have been planted, helping to bind soils and create shade for stream temperature control. Logjams and debris deposited by lahars have been removed to allow migrating fish runs. The Department of Fisheries has begun fish-stocking programs on several rivers.

Plants will continue to invade the area, bringing the mountain slopes alive with splashes of floral color. Wildlife will make their homes on and around the mountain, their young becoming the early colonizers for the more severely disturbed portions of the land, speeding the process of recovery. After all, what we are so lucky to witness is but one segment of the cycle of life—a cycle that has been completed many times in the past.

Aquatic creatures, such as this frog, survived the blast and are repopulating the area

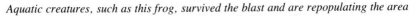

Volcanism

A Fiery Forge

A dormancy of 123 years ended for Mount St. Helens on March 20, 1980, when the volcano began to awake from its slumber. Ensuing eruptive activity, which continues to this date, provides a dramatic and tragic reminder of the awesome destructive power of a volcano. But volcanoes are also beneficial. Eons before the first humans walked on this planet, volcanoes were playing a decisive role in forming and modifying the earth's terrain. Over 80 percent of the earth's surface is of volcanic origin. Millions of years of volcanic eruptions created mountains, plateaus, and plains which have been sculptured by erosional and weathering processes into spectacular landscapes and fertile soils. Also, volcanoes produced gaseous emissions that aided the formation of the earth's atmosphere and water bodies.

In ancient times volcanoes and volcanic eruptions were, and still are in many areas, regarded with fear and awe by the people who witnessed them. Considering the immense displays of power unleashed during a large eruption, it is easy to understand their fears and anxieties. Early societies experienced huge columns of black ash that turned day into night, rainfalls of hot pumice that blanketed surrounding areas, and molten red lava flows that rushed down mountain flanks destroying everything in their paths. It is not surprising that many references to volcanoes are contained in ancient legends and myths; these were attempts of the early peoples to explain and understand the volcanic events they witnessed.

The word "volcano" is derived from the island of Vulcano, located off Sicily in the Mediterranean Sea. Some of the world's most active volcanoes are in this region, accounting for the many myths and names that evolved here concerning these fiery giants.

According to Roman mythology, Vulcan was the god of metal-working. His forge was located beneath the island of Vulcano, where he wrought thunderbolts for Jupiter and weapons for other gods. It was believed that the island of Vulcano was the chimney of Vulcan's forge. Steam and ash emit-

Steam and gas emission from Mount St. Helens, June 1982

41

ting from Vulcano's crater was a sign to surrounding populations that Vulcan was hard at work pounding on his anvil.

Modern scientific knowledge and monitoring techniques have led to greater understanding of the nature of volcanoes, supplying a window to the interior of the globe. Myths and legends from times long past yield an important source of information on the historical activity of volcanoes.

Building of a Volcano

The term "volcano" has a dual definition. It is a "place or opening from which molten rock, tephra (a general term for all air-fall pyroclastics from a volcano), or gas, generally more than one of these, issue from the earth's interior to its surface," and "the hill or mountain built up around the opening (vent) by accumulation of the rock material poured or thrown out." "Volcano" may refer to a vent that spouts gases, tephra, or lava, but has not yet formed a mountain.

Volcanoes are formed differently from other types of mountains. While most topographic features are created by crumpling, folding, uplift, and erosion of the earth's crust, volcanoes are built by the accumulation of their own eruptive products—lava, ash, and tephra.

Single or repeated eruptions occurring from one vent result in localized accumulation of volcanic debris around that particular vent, forming a volcanic cone. Typically a U-shaped depression called a crater occupies the apex or sides of the cone. Numerous examples of cones with craters are found throughout the Cascade Range, extending from Mount Garibaldi in British Columbia to California's Lassen Peak. A larger depression in the volcanic cone is referred to as a caldera and is less common. It is created by the inward collapse of the mountain top, leaving an opening a mile or more wide. The most famous caldera of the Cascades is at Mount Mazama (Crater Lake), Oregon. When violent eruptions about 6,700 years ago hollowed the interior of Mount Mazama, its top collapsed. The resulting caldera measures 5 by 6 miles across and nearly 3,700 vertical feet deep. Many calderas in the world have been filled with water, creating lakes.

During an eruption, ejected rock material may be either fragments of older near-surface rock torn loose and removed by escaping gases or new rock material coming from greater depths beneath the volcano. Rock beneath the surface in liquid form is known as magma, and after being ejected from the volcano it is called lava. The consolidated masses of rock left after the lava has cooled on the land surface are called extrusive rock. But some magma does not escape. It solidifies below the surface, forming intrusive rock.

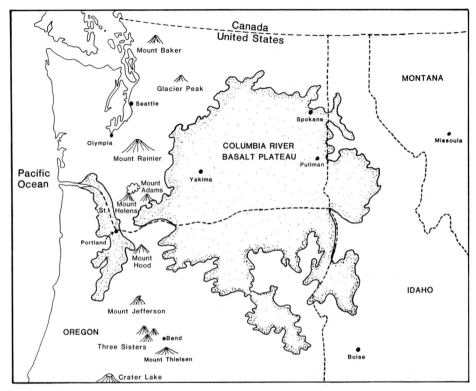

Columbia River Basalt Plateau

Lava may also spout from separate vents (fissures), building enormous lava beds. Depending on whether the eruption takes place at low or high elevations, these lava flows can create plains or plateaus. In the Pacific Northwest, the Columbia River Basalt Plateau and the adjacent Snake River Basalt Plain testify to the huge area lava flows can cover. Columbia River basalts originated between 17 and 6 million years ago, mostly of Miocene Age (Appendix 3) when 11 million years of intensive eruptive activity formed the 50,000-square-mile Columbia River Plateau. Snake River basalts covering an area of about 20,000 square miles were produced several million years later (Quaternary Period), with most activity occurring less than 50,000 years ago to as recently as 2,100 years ago at Craters of the Moon, Idaho. Hundreds of flows, one superimposed on the other, continued to build the Columbia River Plateau and Snake River Plain, to the point where over 70,000 square miles of Washington, Oregon, and Idaho were covered. The volume of lava produced during these eruptions was enormous, estimated at over 100,000 cubic miles. Whereas individual flows averaged 30 to 100 feet thick, combined lava deposits over 3,000 feet deep have been found which actually bury mountain landscapes.

Volcanoes are usually fed from a magma chamber located at a relatively shallow depth beneath the earth's surface. Contained within the chamber are gases under tremendous pressure which drive magma upward toward the surface through a system of channels called conduits. A roughly cylindrical conduit is referred to as a volcanic pipe. Magma often congeals and becomes preserved in the feeding conduits of the volcano. Since magma is more resistant to erosion than the enclosing rock formation, when the volcano becomes inactive years of weathering will expose the "insides" of the volcano. These irregular, columnar structures, which represent the conduit system of the volcano, are known as volcanic plugs or necks. On its course to the surface, magma may follow a more complex conduit system composed of cracks and fissures. As magma solidifies in these fissures to form dikes, the stability of the volcano is greatly enhanced because dikes tend to act as ribs, encircling the volcano and strengthening the volcanic edifice.

Solid fragmentary material released from a volcano is known as pyroclastic material. This term encompasses different forms of volcanic material, from huge chunks of rock through fine dustlike particles suspended in air. Pyroclastic material falls into several categories according to its size and shape. One major category is volcanic bombs. Usually less than a foot across but often reaching a weight of several tons, volcanic bombs are rounded and cooled during their flight through the air from the crater. Some are known as "bread-crust bombs," because the skin is cooled in flight but the interior remains molten much like soft plastic. The continued expansion of internal gases causes the cooled crust to tear open, forming gaping cracks like those of thick-crusted bread.

Bread-crust bomb

Rock fragments the size of a golf ball and smaller are lapilli (from a Latin word meaning "little stones"), cinders, and ash. The term "ash" is misleading, since it implies that it is a product of burning. Ash is simply pulverized rock ground up by rapidly expanding gases or by collision with other material in flight.

Another type of material produced during an eruption is pumice. Often the gas content in pyroclastic material is so high that the magma tends to "froth" as it surges upward in the conduit. When it breaks to the surface, there may be violent separations of the gases from lava, yielding a rapidly cooling froth called pumice. It can range in size from pumiceous ash and lapilli to as big as a foot or more in diameter, yet because of gas bubbles it is often light enough to float on water.

To many people, the first product that comes to mind when thinking of a volcanic eruption is lava. A vision of red-hot lava flowing down upon a city and its terrified population is very common. Fortunately, not all lava acts this way. The chemical composition of a lava, especially the percentage of silicon dioxide, commonly referred to as silica, is critical in determining its type and texture. Geologists have divided volcanic rock into four major groupings according to silica content: basalt (45 to 54 percent), andesite (54 to 63 percent), dacite (63 to 69 percent), and rhyolite (69 percent or more). Highly viscous or thick lavas such as dacites and rhyolites are rich in silica and do not allow gases to move freely within them. In these lavas a great amount of pressure builds up, which is ultimately released in an explosive eruption. The gases in this kind of lava might be compared to gases in a bottle of champagne. If one places a thumb over the top of the bottle and shakes it vigorously, gas will separate from the liquid, forming bubbles. When the thumb is quickly removed, a small eruption of gas and liquid will result.

Large piece of pumice ejected from Mount St. Helens

Obviously on a much greater scale, gases contained in high-silica lavas will react in much the same way. When released from the volcano, gases will violently blast out masses of solid and molten rock. The cataclysmic 1980 lateral eruption of Mount St. Helens was produced in this way.

Lavas with relatively low percentages of silica (basalts) allow gases to escape easily, resulting in relatively passive but spectacular eruptions. Basalt lava will run freely at speeds of !0 to 25 mph, forming long, wide, and thick flows. Generally, basalt flows are of two types, for which the Hawaiian names of aa [aa'-ah] and pahoehoe [pa-ho'y-hoy] are used. Aa lava flows appear as a mass of angular, jagged blocks with a rough, rubbly surface. Flows of pahoehoe lava look quite different. The smooth outer surface has the appearance of huge coils of rope. Examples of basaltic lava flows can be found at the Hawaiian volcanoes of Kilauea and Mauna Loa. Mount St. Helens produced a basalt flow about 1,900 years ago; evidence of it can be seen at Ape Cave and Lava Casts interpretive sites.

Plate Tectonics and the Ring of Fire

To understand why volcanoes are distributed as they are around the world, it is necessary to examine other major features of the earth's crust. The earth's surface is divided into land and seas, continents and oceans. This division, however, is not a result of mere chance but occurred because of the process of plate tectonics.

Aa basalt lava flow from base of Lava Butte. Note lava blister (tumulus) at right, formed when lava solidified around a gas bubble

Pahoehoe lava. Ripple pattern indicates that the flow moves from left to right

It is hypothesized that about 200 million years ago all the land masses on earth made up one supercontinent named Pangaea. This huge land mass was surrounded by Panthalassa, the ancestral Pacific Ocean. By the end of the Triassic period, 180 million years ago, Pangaea had separated into two enormous continents: Laurasia to the north, Gondwanaland to the south. These continued to fragment, resulting in separate land masses which drifted over the last 180 million years to the present location of today's continents. The Atlantic and Indian oceans, formed where continents once split apart, grow larger in size as continents slowly drift apart. The Pacific Ocean, pressed on all sides by drifting continents, is shrinking.

According to the currently accepted theory of plate tectonics, the lithosphere—the rigid outer shell of the earth—is broken into about a dozen major shifting slabs or plates, averaging 50 miles in thickness, upon which the continents are firmly attached. These slabs slowly migrate across the surface of the planet and interact with other plates in a number of ways. Two plates may pull apart from each other (sea floor spreading), creating a rift where magma upwells, cools, and adds new surface to the lithosphere, such as the Mid-Atlantic Rift. This rift is part of a continuous mountain range that twists and branches some 40,000 miles through the earth's ocean floors. Opposite movements will find two plates converging and colliding, and owing to the pressures of such movement, one plate typically descends beneath another at what is called the subduction zone. Plates may also slide in opposite directions alongside each other, neither creating nor destroying lithosphere. At margins of converging plates where crust is being consumed, there are three common types of interaction. The first is oceanic against continental (Pacific Basin and South American plates); the second is oceanic against oceanic (as illustrated by the western two-thirds of the Aleutian arc); and the third is continental against continental (the Himalayas at the conjunction of the Indian and Eurasian plates.) These slowly migrating plates have changed and renewed the face of the earth over hundreds of millions of years and continue as a vital process.

Since continental plates are thicker and more stable than oceanic plates, the oceanic plate is forced under the continental plate. At the line of initial subduction, deep oceanic trenches and volcanic mountain ranges are formed. Finally, the descending lithosphere is assimilated into the earth's mantle. A good example of subduction is along the western edge of the North American Plate. The oceanic Juan de Fuca Plate is thrusting under the continental North American Plate at the rate of an inch per year. At depths of about 60 to 80 miles along the zone of contact between the descending lithosphere and overriding plate, rocks are melted to form magma, which rises through the North American Plate and is erupted to form the volcanoes of the Cascade Range. This process explains why chains of volcanoes border almost the entire circumference of the Pacific Ocean Basin.

More than 500 volcanoes throughout the world have been documented as having erupted at least once in the last 400 years. Fifty of these are located

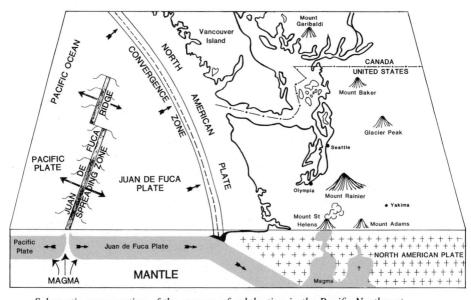

Schematic cross section of the process of subduction in the Pacific Northwest

in Hawaii, Alaska, Washington, Oregon, and California. Most of these active volcanoes, including Mount St. Helens, are called plate-boundary volcanoes, and tend to cluster along narrow mountain belts where folding and fracturing are severe.

The Pacific Ocean Basin contains the boundaries of several plates, which form a somewhat circular area of connected islands, peninsulas, and continental margins. More than half of the world's active volcanoes are located on or near its borders. Called the Ring of Fire, the Pacific Ocean Basin is an example of plate-boundary volcano formation.

In extensive studies, scientists have examined the volcanoes along plate interaction zones. These zones provide weakened areas in the earth's crust where magma is able to escape to the surface. Major earthquake zones also tend to be centered along these mountain belts at plate boundaries. Most of these earthquakes are generated as one plate slides beneath another.

In contrast to plate-boundary volcanoes, intra-plate volcanoes are situated away from plate boundaries. These volcanoes form roughly linear chains in the interior of oceanic plates. In the Hawaiian islands, for example, as the northwest-moving Pacific Plate passes over a supposed hot spot beneath the ocean floor, eruptive processes are initiated.

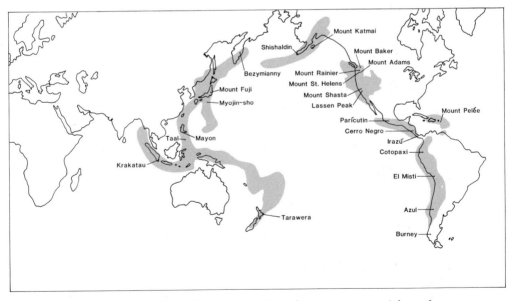

Areas of earthquake activity (shaded) and major volcanic areas on periphery of Pacific Ocean

Birth of the Cascade Range

The present Cascade topography of dagger-sharp peaks, jagged ridges, and deep gorges is the result of millions of years of weathering, erosion, and glaciation. Beginning at the rugged Sierra Nevada of California near Lassen Peak, the Cascade mountain range extends to the moist Coast Range of British Columbia. The magnificent Cascades range from 30 to 50 miles wide in the south to well over 80 miles across in the glaciated wilderness of northern Washington. Cascade peaks average 4,500 to 5,000 feet high in the southern region, with scores of peaks towering in excess of 8,000 feet in the north. Built upon this mountainous base are individual volcanic cones born through thousands of years of eruptive activity.

The Cascades are thought to be one of the most geologically complex mountain ranges in the world. This is because the mountains we view today are relatively new, overlaid upon an older, ancestral range. During the late Paleozoic and early Mesozoic eras, most of the area now occupied by the Cascade Range was covered by a marine environment. Sediments and volcanic rock accumulated on the ancient sea floor. During the Cretaceous period, this seabed was uplifted and, through a series of folding and thrusting processes, was formed into the ancestral Cascade Range, complete with active volcanoes. The alignment of this ancient range was in a northwest-southeast direction. As the process of uplift slowed, the forces of weathering and erosion began to tear down the range, and by the late Miocene epoch, the ancestral Cascades had been reduced to low, smooth hills.

During the late Tertiary period, probably about 10 to 15 million years ago, a renewed episode of uplift produced the present Cascade Range, oriented on a north-south axis. Since uplifting progressed slowly, existing drainage patterns of the ancestral range were maintained. There was enough time for rivers to cut channels in the uplifted material without having to change from their original courses. Cascade streams and rivers continue to flow northwest or southeast as they did millions of years ago.

Uplift continued into the Quaternary period, accompanied by increased volcanism and glaciation. Volcanic eruptions built towering cones such as Mount St. Helens on top of the existing Cascades while great ice sheets moved down from the north. During the Pleistocene epoch (Ice Age), at least four advances and retreats of ice scoured virtually all of British Columbia and the northern areas of Washington, Idaho, and Montana. At this time, a scene reminiscent of Antarctica, where only the highest peaks pierce the great ice sheets, existed in the Pacific Northwest. A great tongue of ice, known as the Puget Lobe, spread south from British Columbia across the Puget lowland to as far as Olympia, Washington. About 15,000 to 13,000 years ago, the last of these great glacial advances, the Fraser Glaciation, covered the area of present-day Seattle under about 4,000 feet of ice. During this period of ice advance, alpine glaciers also increased in size. Rivers of ice produced U-shaped valleys and glacial basins typical of the North Cascades. Prior to glaciation, the new Cascade Range looked much like today's Great Smoky Mountains in North Carolina and Tennessee. The advance of alpine glaciers eroded and shaped the overlying smooth layers into razor-sharp peaks and rugged ridge lines.

Alpine glaciation had little influence on the topography of the South Cascades because of their lower elevations. Cascade volcanoes, including Mount St. Helens, were an important exception. Because of the volcanoes' great height, massive alpine glaciers were able to exist on their slopes. Over a lengthy span of years, periodic eruptions added volcanic material to the mountain flanks, repairing damage caused by the carving effects of alpine glaciers. The greater the frequency of eruptions, the more smooth and symmetrical the volcano's slopes would appear. Mount St. Helens, before its 1980 eruptions, was a classic example of a volcano in constant repair. In contrast is Mount Adams, 40 miles east of Mount St. Helens, whose deeply carved slopes indicate little recent volcanic activity.

The last major glacial advance, known as the Fraser Glaciation, ended approximately 8,000 to 10,000 years ago, marking the end of the great Pleistocene epoch. For the next 4,000 years the climate warmed, forcing the ice sheets to retreat. Most of the alpine glaciers disappeared during this warming trend, and the Cascade Range lost its mantling of snow and ice.

During the postglacial period, over the last 5,000 to 3,000 years, at least two episodes of cooling recurred, causing reestablishment of glaciers in the Cascades. This trend of slightly cooler temperatures has allowed the return of alpine glaciers, especially on shaded north and east slopes. These alpine glaciers are only a small remnant of the once great rivers of ice that covered this land.

Cascade Volcanoes

Cinder Cones

The simplest type of volcano is a cinder cone. These symmetrical cones build up at a single vent site where particles and globules of molten lava are ejected into the air. During an eruption, gas-charged lava is blown out of the vent, shattering into rock fragments of various sizes. Coarser material solidifies in flight and falls back around the vent, forming a circular or oval cone with smooth slopes of about 30 degrees. Finer material may settle around the vent or be transported many miles by wind. Most cinder cones have a bowl-shaped crater at their summit and rarely exceed 1,000 feet above surrounding terrain. Wizard Island in Crater Lake and Lava Butte in the Oregon Cascades are good examples of cinder cones.

Shield Volcanoes

Initial activity during the late Pliocene, followed by intense volcanic activity in the Pleistocene epoch, 2 to 3 million years ago, created numerous shield volcanoes in and around the Cascade Range. Located in northern California and in Oregon, these shields are 3 to 4 miles in diameter and from 1,500 to 2,000 feet high. Having been extinct for thousands of years, most Cascade shields are extensively eroded, exposing the volcanic material solidified in their conduits. Reminders of their glorious past, only lava plugs remain at Mount Washington, Mount Thielsen, Union Peak, and Three Fingered Jack, located in southern and central Oregon. One of the best-preserved shields is central Oregon's Newberry Volcano, with a base diameter of 20 miles. Located about 40 miles east of the Cascade chain, Newberry's summit cone has slumped to form a huge caldera 4 by 5 miles across, something that happens to many large shield volcanoes.

Typical shield volcanoes are built almost entirely of successive flows of extremely hot basaltic lava. During an eruption, fluid lava issues from one or more vents and spreads over great distances before solidifying. The characteristic shape of a shield volcano is a gently sloped, broad cone whose flanks seldom exceed 10 degrees in steepness. The term "shield volcano" is used because these volcanoes resemble a warrior's shield lying face up on the ground.

At times, shield volcanoes release lava so fluid that no cone is built at all. When lava erupts from fissures instead of central vents, the surrounding countryside may be flooded with flow after flow, forming vast lava plateaus and plains. The Columbia River Basalt Plateau and Snake River Basalt Plain were developed by numerous fissure eruptions of this sort.

The most impressive aspect of shield volcanoes is their immense size. Some of the world's largest and most active volcanoes are of the shield type, such as Kilauea and Mauna Loa in Hawaii. The size of these volcanoes is deceptive because only the portion above sea level is visible. But when the ocean depth at Hawaii of 15,000 feet is added to Mauna Loa's elevation of 13,677 feet above sea level, its tremendous height of nearly 29,000 feet makes it the largest active shield in the world. The width of the Hawaiian Island shield complex at its base is over 1,000 miles.

Wizard Island (cinder cone) surrounded by Crater Lake and the caldera rim of Mount Mazama (composite volcano)

Lava Butte, a basalt cinder (scoria) cone south of Bend, Oregon. Formed 5,000 to 6,000 years ago by a pyroclastic eruption

View from southwest rim of Newberry Volcano, northeast caldera rim in distance. Note two lakes, which are old craters, and pumice cones between lakes. Old obsidian flow in foreground was erupted 1,350 years ago

Composite Volcanoes

Composite volcanoes, also known as stratovolcanoes, are among the most breathtaking mountains in the world. They are typically steep-sided with symmetrical cones of large dimensions, and are higher and steeper than shield volcanoes. Composite volcanoes consist of alternating layers of lava flows (usually andesite) and pyroclastic material that has fallen or flowed onto the slopes during an eruption, and intrusive lava domes (commonly visible as knobs, such as Dog's Head on Mount St. Helens).

All of the loftiest peaks in the Cascade Range, including Mount St. Helens, are composite volcanoes. Mount Rainier of Washington, at the height of 14,410 feet, towers above the landscape, rising nearly 8,000 feet higher than surrounding peaks.

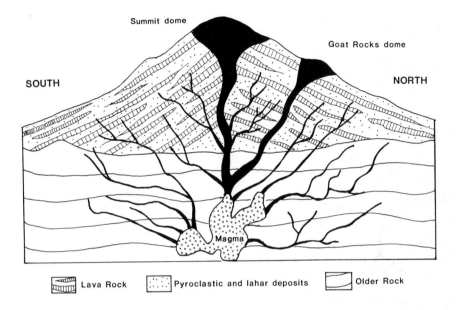

Composite volcano

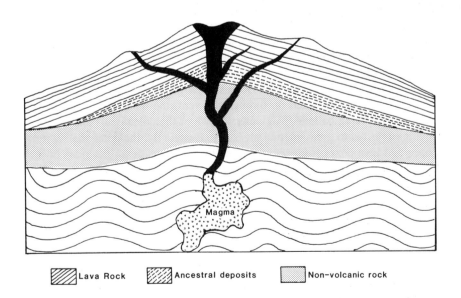

Shield volcano

Table 1. Eruptive History of Mount St. Helens (a = andesite, b = basalt, d = dacite)

Eruptive Periods	Approx. No. of Years Ago	Tephra Unit	Eruptive Products
Goat Rocks	150–100	T(d)	Dome building (d) Lava flows (a)
Kalama	450–350	X(a) W(d)	Pyroclastic flows (d, a) Dome building (d) Lava flows (a)
Sugar Bowl	1,150		Dome building (d) Pyroclastic flows (d) Lateral blast (d)
Castle Creek	>2,200–1,700	B(b,a,d)	Lava flows (a,b) Pyroclastic flows (a,d)
Pine Creek	3,000–2,500	P(d)	Pyroclastic flows (d) Dome building (d)
Smith Creek	4,000–3,300	Y(d)	Pyroclastic flows (d)
Swift Creek	13,000–>8,000	J(d) S(d)	Pyroclastic flows (d) Dome building (d)
Cougar	20,000–18,000	K(d) M(d)	Pyroclastic flows (d) Dome building (d) Lava flows (d)
Ape Canyon	~40,000(?)–~35,000	C(d)	Pyroclastic flows (d)

NOTE: Lahars were produced during many of these eruptive periods but are not shown here. Some of the tephra unit letters indicate color or location where the tephra layer was first observed: T (Timberline), W (white), B (brown), P (Pine Creek), Y (yellow). Other tephra unit labels (X, J, etc.) have been assigned arbitrarily and have no real significance. Data from Lipman and Mullineaux 1981.

various dating methods, these volcanic remnants indicate that the eruptive history of Mount St. Helens began about 40,000 years ago with dacitic volcanism. Weathered lahar deposits, which formed as torrential flows of water-saturated volcanic debris swept down the slopes of Mount St. Helens, can be found dating nearly 36,000 years of age. Old Mount St. Helens intermittently produced eruptions of air-fall tephra (ash) plus flows of hot gases and pyroclastic debris. These eruptive periods, which lasted hundreds to thousands of years, were separated by dormant periods of a few hundred to about 15,000 years.

Several of the more recent eruptive periods were significant enough to deserve discussion.

Smith Creek Eruptive Period

Several of the largest explosive eruptions in Mount St. Helens's history occurred sometime between 4,000 and 3,300 years ago, forming the "Y" (for yellow) tephra deposits. The deposits indicate at least ten separate eruptions. This yellowish-brown pumice produced by these larger eruptions can easily be found today. At Mount Rainier National Park, 50 miles from Mount St. Helens, Yn (for yellow north) deposits are up to 18 inches thick, and small amounts of Yn have been found as far as Banff Park, in Alberta, Canada. The total volume of volcanic material ejected by Y eruptions was about 1.0 cubic mile, compared with less than 0.1 cubic mile (not including avalanche and lahar deposits) produced on May 18, 1980 (see table 2).

Successive eruptions during the Smith Creek Eruptive Period produced lahars and pyroclastic flows that broadened the base of the mountain over a period of centuries. An ancestor of Spirit Lake probably came into existence at this time as lahar and pyroclastic flow deposits dammed the North Fork Toutle River.

Castle Creek Eruptive Period

One of the most interesting features about Mount St. Helens's geologic history is the change in eruptive behavior around 2,200 years ago. The prior 38,000 years were characterized by eruptions of dacite. Then, for reasons not known, basalt and andesite began to alternate with dacite. Streams of basalt lava flowed eight to ten miles down the south and east flanks of the mountain, pouring into the canyon of the Lewis River and headwaters of the Kalama River. These basaltic eruptions produced an extensive system of lava tubes, of which the best known is Ape Cave.

Kalama Eruptive Period

Occurring 450 to 350 years ago, the Kalama Eruptive Period was characterized by explosive activity that generated large amounts of pumice, lapilli,

Table 2. Estimated Volume of Ejecta during Historical Eruptions

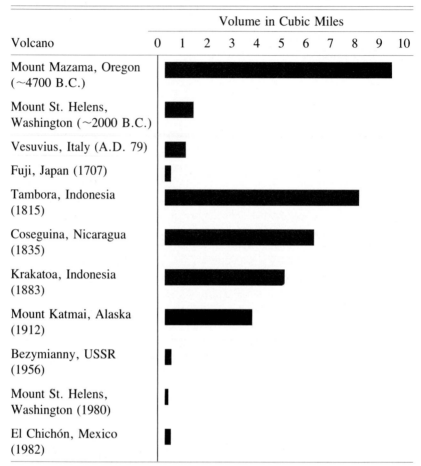

Volcano	Volume in Cubic Miles
Mount Mazama, Oregon (~4700 B.C.)	~9
Mount St. Helens, Washington (~2000 B.C.)	~1
Vesuvius, Italy (A.D. 79)	~1
Fuji, Japan (1707)	<1
Tambora, Indonesia (1815)	~8
Coseguina, Nicaragua (1835)	~6
Krakatoa, Indonesia (1883)	~5
Mount Katmai, Alaska (1912)	~4
Bezymianny, USSR (1956)	<1
Mount St. Helens, Washington (1980)	<1
El Chichón, Mexico (1982)	<1

NOTE: This comparison vividly shows how small the May 1980 eruption of Mount St. Helens was. If there had not been the huge debris avalanche which released the devastating lateral blast, much of the surrounding landscape would not have been affected. Data from Foxworthy and Hill 1982, Bullard 1976, MacDonald 1972.

and ash (andesite and dacite). These eruptions, known as the "W" (for white), were the most violent since the Y eruptions. Today, a whitish pumice layer several feet thick can be found many miles northeast of Mount St. Helens. The large dacite dome that formed most of the pre–May 18, 1980, summit of the volcano had been formed during the later stages of the Kalama Eruptive Period.

Prior to the May 18, 1980, eruption, the most recent damming and deepening of Spirit Lake occurred during the Kalama Eruptive Period, with the lake's level rising at least 60 feet.

Goat Rocks Eruptive Period

In the fall of 1799 or spring of 1800, Mount St. Helens again spread large amounts of pumice over a wide area. The "T" layer (for Timberline) was deposited up to several feet thick on the northeast slopes of the volcano. Winds blowing in that direction carried ash for hundreds of miles over central and eastern Washington, northern Idaho, western Montana, and even parts of Canada. The Floating Island Lava Flow (andesite) and Goat Rocks dacite dome were formed during this eruptive period. Small-scale steam explosions were observed in 1898, 1903, and 1921; none produced appreciable deposits of debris.

Cultural Setting

Native American History

Who Were the People

It is unclear which Native American groups inhabited areas of southwestern Washington near Mount St. Helens before the arrival of Euroamericans to the Pacific Northwest. Almost certainly the land was occupied by at least 10,000 years ago and quite possibly two to three times that long. Human occupation sites found on the Northwest Coast are from 10,000 to 12,000 years old, so it is reasonable to assume that people were present in the St. Helens area. But little archaeological evidence has come to light from this region. Repeated deposition of volcanic material over the span of centuries has concealed much of the archaeological evidence dealing with old village and seasonal sites. Also, since Native Americans generally lived in small, widely scattered family groups with few possessions, little evidence is likely to have been left. Therefore, the ethnographic sketch presented can only be based on information received from later white contact.

At the time of the first Euroamerican contact, the two most prominent Native American groups using resources in the vicinity of the mountain were the Cowlitz and Klickitat.

The Cowlitz can be divided into four separate groups—Lower, Mountain, Lewis River, and Upper—based on their geographical, historical, and linguistic differences. There were no well-defined boundary lines separating these Cowlitz groups. Every Cowlitz individual had full freedom to move from one group to another. The Cowlitz ranged eastward to the crest of the Cascade Range and to the Willapa Hills in the west, northerly to the divide between the Chehalis, Deschutes, and Cowlitz rivers, and to near the Columbia River in the south. The Cowlitz were (and are) an inland people related to a broad Salishan-speaking group who occupied most of western Washing-

Fire lookout on Mount St. Helens's summit built in 1916 (later abandoned in favor of lower-elevation sites)

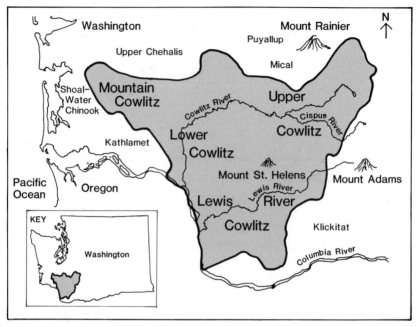

Area inhabited by Cowlitz Native Americans

ton. Klickitat were (and are) Sahaptin speakers who were principally found in the valleys between Mount St. Helens and Mount Adams. Over the years the two cultures slowly merged as trading links across the mountains strengthened.

Before Euroamericans arrived in the Pacific Northwest, land and resources near Mount St. Helens were probably shared by various Native American groups. Evidence indicates, however, that the Cowlitz were probably the earliest inhabitants of the area.

The Cowlitz

The highly specialized subsistence pattern of the Cowlitz was based on a seasonal procurement of food that began about the first of May when the Cowlitz left their villages and traveled north to several large prairies near the Cowlitz River. After setting up temporary lodges, they turned their efforts to root digging and hunting. Camas bulbs and other wild roots such as wapato, carrots, and onions were unearthed, and were either cooked for immediate use or preserved for winter consumption.

Yakima woman drying berries in 1932 near Mount Adams

Spring marked the beginning of trade between the various Cowlitz groups, who met to exchange fish and game. The Upper Cowlitz capitalized on elk, deer, bear, mountain sheep, and goats, which inhabited high country areas near their Cascade upland villages, while the Lower Cowlitz concentrated on the smelt runs. This exchange not only provided each group with a good portion of the protein needed for the winter months but also reinforced intergroup bonds through the transfer of ideas and bloodlines.

With the approach of late summer the Cowlitz left the wide prairies and traveled to traditional berry-picking sites. Here extended families gathered in a festive mood to share news and stories from the previous year. This was a busy time for the Cowlitz, as men set out in search of game and fish while women combed mountain meadows gathering berries, which they prepared for winter storage. For relaxation, the Cowlitz participated in horse racing, gambling, and feasted on berries, fish, and meat.

Native American campsite in 1932

As fall approached, families returned to their villages to prepare dwellings for the oncoming winter, and to take advantage of the salmon runs in the lower rivers and streams. Fish were dried and mixed with berries into pemmican, or smoked over alderwood fires, a tradition that survives to this day.

In winter the Cowlitz settled into their secured longhouses. The adequate provisions of food and other necessary items allowed them to turn their attention to the education of their children and to winter rites which perpetuated traditions of the tribe. With the passage of each winter day, the Cowlitz looked ahead to spring and their return to the large prairies to resume the seasonal cycle.

Recent History

At their peak, it is estimated that over 4,000 Cowlitz inhabited areas in the vicinity of the Lower Cowlitz River. During the winter of 1829–30 nearly 80 percent of the Cowlitz were killed by the European-introduced "intermittent fever" plague, to which many Native American groups had little resistance. The rapid depopulation of the Cowlitz produced social disarray as well as individual and family suffering beyond description. After 1830, the Klickitat apparently moved westward over the Cascades in great numbers, taking advantage of the Cowlitz and other southwest Washington Native American groups. By the mid-19th century, large tracts of land once occupied by the Cowlitz were under the control of the Klickitat.

In 1853, Isaac I. Stevens (1818–62) was appointed governor of the Territory of Washington and superintendent of Indian Affairs, and was responsible for negotiating treaties between the U.S. government and Native American groups in the Washington Territory. In southwest Washington, a proposed treaty called for a 640-acre parcel set aside on the Cowlitz River for the Cowlitz, but this was never ratified. In 1855, a new treaty was offered to the Cowlitz and other local groups which would relocate them to a single reservation between Grays Harbor and Cape Flattery on the Washington coast. Although some groups accepted the terms of this treaty, the Cowlitz refused to sign because they were unwilling to move to a coastal reservation away from their ancestral homeland, to live with those who were not kin.

In 1973, the Cowlitz were awarded $1,550,000 for all their previous territory, even though they had never received federal recognition as the Cowlitz Indian Tribe. To this day they continue to petition the secretary of interior for federal recognition.

Hostilities among Native American groups in the eastern portion of the territory were more difficult to resolve. The impact on tribal lands of set-

Native American women often strapped baskets to their bodies to free their hands for faster picking

tlers, who were seen as trespassers by Native Americans, led to the Indian Wars of 1855–58. Settlers were ambushed and killed. Alarmed by these occurrences, Indian Agent A. J. Bolon was sent to investigate. He too was killed, and as a result several companies of troops were sent into tribal lands to put down the uprising. On several encounters the troops were decisively beaten by the warring Native American groups. Although most of the conflict was on the eastern side of the Cascades, encounters did occur on the west side. One of the more colorful accounts tells of an incident that took place near Mount St. Helens at Chelatchie Prairie (site of the Mount St. Helens National Volcanic Monument Headquarters). On the evening of March 28, 1856, "Indian Zack," a friend to the settlers, was hunting in the prairie when he spotted about two hundred Yakima and Klickitat warriors camped in the area, preparing to raid settlers. Indian Zack ran down the valley echoing the alarm, allowing settlers time to escape.

More troops were sent into eastern portions of the territory. Horses used by the Native Americans were rounded up and slaughtered and their stores of winter food were destroyed. Native Americans were soon scattered, dispirited, and in poverty. Sporadic fighting continued until late in 1858, when Native Americans began to surrender. On April 18, 1859, a treaty was ratified by President Buchanan establishing three reservations in the eastern part of the territory where indigenous groups were relocated, thus ending hostilities.

Native American Legends and Eruptive Accounts

Mount St. Helens is the heroine of many Native American legends. One of the most interesting is the "Bridge of the Gods" story. According to one version of this legend, a mighty land bridge once spanned the river known today as the Columbia near the present town of Cascade Locks. Kept on this bridge was the sacred fire—the only fire in the world. Native Americans from all parts came to the bridge to borrow fire. Faithfully guarding the fire was a wrinkled old witch named Loo-wit-lat-kla, "Lady of Fire," who had been given the gift of eternal life by Sahale, the great chief. Sahale had also bestowed this gift upon his sons Klickitat and Wyeast, who ruled, respectively, territories to the north and south of the bridge.

Loo-wit's gift of eternal life saddened her, because she did not want to live forever as an ugly old witch. Her sadness was of great concern to Sahale, whose gift of eternal life could not be retracted. Sahale therefore granted

Mount Adams (Klickitat) and Mount Hood (Wyeast) from the summit of Mount Rainier (Tahoma)

Loo-wit a wish of her choice, and she immediately requested to be young and beautiful. Instantly Loo-wit was transformed into a maiden of incomparable loveliness. The fame of Loo-wit's beauty spread quickly, and both Klickitat and Wyeast fell hopelessly in love with her and she with them. But Loo-wit was indecisive and could not choose between them. To win her, Klickitat and Wyeast waged a war against each other that resulted in widespread death and destruction. Sadly, Sahale watched as his sons fought over their desired love. Eventually he became so angry that he destroyed the great bridge, causing it to crumble into the river—forming the Cascade Rapids. Sahale was not satisfied, however, so he smote the three lovers and reared mighty volcanic peaks where they fell. Lovely Loo-wit became the beautiful Mount St. Helens; Wyeast, who was full of dignity, became the proud standing Mount Hood; while Klickitat, who had a tender heart, became Mount Adams, with his head forever bowed in sorrow as he gazes down on Loo-wit in all her beauty.

The first published reference to volcanic activity that had occurred at Mount St. Helens prior to the appearance of European or American explorers was recorded in June 1841 by naval Lieutenant Robert E. Johnson. As Johnson was interviewing Cornelius (or Bighead), the nearly sixty-year-old chief of the Spokane Indians, events of "some fifty years ago" became vividly clear. Cornelius recalled that when he was about ten years old he had been sleeping in a lodge with a large group of people when he "was suddenly awakened by his mother, who called out to him that the world was falling to pieces. He then heard a great noise of thunder overhead, and all the people crying out in terror. Something was falling very thick, which they at first took for snow, but on going out they found it to be dirt: it proved to be ashes, which fell to the depth of six inches, and increased their fears, by causing them to suppose that the end of the world was actually at hand'' (Wilkes).

In 1861 a story entitled ''Gold Hunting in the Cascade Mountains,'' by a pseudonymous author Loo-Wit Lat-Kla, appeared in the Vancouver *Weekly Chronicle*. The article described an ascent of Mount St. Helens by the author and his companions lead by Native American guides. At one point during the climb the guides stopped talking and began indicating climbing routes up the mountain by pointing with their gunsticks. Well short of the summit the guides stopped altogether, forcing the climbing party to complete the ascent on their own. It was only after their return to the base of Mount St. Helens that the author discovered the reasons for the guides' peculiar actions: ''They afterwards told us that they had too much reverence of the Spirit, and were too much awed by this evidence of His mighty power, to laugh and talk foolishly in the sight of Him who had devastated the traditional hunting grounds of their fathers'' (Loo-Wit Lat-Kla).

Published legends along with Native American lore later passed on to European and American explorers strongly suggest that Native Americans who lived in the shadows of these towering volcanoes regarded them with awe.

Exploration and Settlement

First Sightings

On May 19, 1792, the famed English naval explorer George Vancouver (1757–98) made the first recorded sighting of Mount St. Helens. Vancouver was in the area searching for the fabled Northwest Passage through the North American continent. His exhaustive exploration of the Northwest Coast (1792–94) confirmed that no such passage existed.

Vancouver was in the process of mapping inlets of Puget Sound on May 19, 1792. Shortly before noon he guided his ship, *Discovery,* to waters off the present-day site of Fort Lawton in Seattle. The cloudless sky offered an unobstructed panorama to the southeast, where the ship's crew viewed a beautiful volcano: ''I continued our course up the main inlet, which now extended as far as, from the deck, the eye could reach, though, from the mast-head, intervening land appeared, beyond which another high round mountain (Mount St. Helens) covered with snow was discovered, apparently situated several leagues to the south of mount Rainier, and bearing by compass S. 22 E. This I considered as a further extension of the eastern snowy range; but the intermediate mountains, connecting it with mount Rainier, were not sufficiently high to be seen at that distance'' (Vancouver).

Most likely because of poor visibility in the area, Mount St. Helens was not mentioned again by Vancouver until the autumn of 1792, when the *Discovery* sailed toward California. On October 20, while pausing off the Columbia River, Vancouver again sighted and then named (Native Americans already had many names for Mount St. Helens) the white-capped volcano: ''The clearness of the atmosphere enabled us to see the high round snowy mountain (Mount St. Helens), noticed when in the southern parts of Admiralty inlet, to the southward of mount Rainier; from this station it bore by compass N. 77 E., and, like mount Rainier, seemed covered with perpetual snow, as low down as the intervening country permitted it to be seen. This I have distinguished by the name of Mount St. Helens, in honor of his Brittanic Majesty's ambassador at the court of Madrid. It is situated in latitude 46 degrees 9', and in longitude 238 degrees 4', according to our observations'' (Vancouver).

Like Mount Rainier, Mount Adams, and Mount Hood, Mount St. Helens honors a man who never set foot in the Northwest. Alleyne Fitzherbert (1753–1839) served as British diplomat to Spain and played a key role in settling differences between those two countries regarding claims of sovereignty to the Northwest Coast. His successful diplomacy earned him high esteem from his government and the title Lord Fitzherbert, baron of St. Helens.

St. Helens had a long and illustrious career in foreign affairs representing the United Kingdom in Germany, France, Spain, and Russia. He was also instrumental in negotiating a peace settlement with the American colonies. Among his many distinctions, St. Helens was a trustee of the British Museum and senior member of the privy council. After retiring from diplomatic life on April 5, 1803, he resided in his beloved London for the duration of his life. Since he had never married, the title baron of St. Helens was discontinued upon his death on February 19, 1839.

The next references concerning Mount St. Helens are found in the journals of Meriwether Lewis (1774–1809) and William Clark (1770–1838), written during their famous 1804–6 journey across the North American continent. On November 4, 1805, while traveling by canoe near the mouth of the Willamette River, Clark took note of the majestic peak: ''Mount Hellen bears N.25 degrees E. about 80 miles. this is the mountain we saw near the forks of this river. it is emensely high and covered with snow, riseing in a kind of cone perhaps the highest pinecal from the common leavel in America. . . . This is the mountain I saw from the Muscle Shell rapid on the 19th of October last covered with Snow, it rises Something in the form of a Sugar lofe'' (Lewis and Clark).

The symmetrical grace of Mount St. Helens made a lasting impression on Clark. In his daily journal of May 30, 1806, he again wrote exuberantly about the mountain's grandeur: "we had a view of mount St. helines and Mount Hood. the 1st, is the most noble looking object of its kind in nature" (Lewis and Clark).

During the early part of the 19th century, increasing numbers of trappers infiltrated the backcountry of the Pacific Northwest in search of valuable pelts. Undoubtedly these trappers were afforded breathtaking views of Mount St. Helens, although only a few casual references about the volcano appear in their journals. One exception is the journal of William Fraser Tolmie (1812–86), a Hudson's Bay Company physician at Fort Nisqually. Much as William Clark was impressed by the elegance of Mount St. Helens, so was Tolmie: "had some fine glimpses of Mount St. Helens—its summit is conical and sides more rounded than those of Mt. Hood. It is invested with a pure sheet of snow, unspotted either by rock or tree, and as seen in relief against the deep azure sky immediately over a gloomy ridge of pine trees in the foreground produced a fine effect" (Tolmie).

Opening of the Pacific Northwest

During the late 18th and early 19th centuries, the strategic and economic significance of the Pacific Northwest came to the attention of European and American governments and business enterprises. As information from government and private expeditions filtered back to settlements, a picture of a wondrous land teeming with mineral, fish, and wildlife resources began to develop. This information sparked the interest that lead to the exploration of the Pacific Northwest and the ultimate settlement of the Mount St. Helens area.

By 1811, the American-owned Pacific Fur Company had established a shipping post called Fort Astoria at the mouth of the Columbia River. This company was sold to the British-based North West Company in 1813, during the outbreak of war between the United States and England. Soon a broad network of forts and outposts appeared throughout much of the Northwest, establishing a vital flow of fur and trade goods. With the 1821 merger of the North West Company into the Hudson's Bay Company, and subsequent removal of company headquarters from the mouth of the Columbia upriver to Fort Vancouver, the British monopolized a fur trade market of huge proportions. The extent of their control was greatly reduced when the Hudson's Bay Company withdrew its main operations northward to Vancouver Island after the establishment of the 49th parallel as the boundary between British territory and the continental United States in June 1846.

Fort Vancouver, the northwest "capitol" of the Hudson's Bay Company, 1845

The Coming of American Settlers

Although thousands of settlers and missionaries had traveled along the Oregon Trail to the Columbia Basin, this area was not officially a territory of the United States until the passage of the "Oregon Territory" bill in 1848. Settlers who had homesteaded north of the Columbia River soon became disgruntled because of their distance from Oregon City, where territorial decisions were made. On August 29, 1851, about a dozen men held a meeting at the house of John R. Jackson (now a historic site one mile north of the National Volcanic Monument Visitor Center) to decide whether to petition for separation from the Oregon Territory. In October 1852, a convention at Monticello (the present Longview) drafted a resolution which was sent to the U.S. Congress requesting the creation of the "territory of Columbia." Changing the name from Columbia to Washington, an act signed by President Fillmore in 1853 created the "Washington Territory." To speed settlement of the region, the Donation Land Act of 1850 enabled single persons to claim 320 acres while couples could claim up to 640 acres.

Greater access to the territory, including areas around Mount St. Helens, occurred with the construction of the Northern Pacific Railroad in the 1870s. This allowed expanded use of the area's available resources, particularly timber, mineral, and agricultural.

Settlement Around Mount St. Helens

By the 1880s a number of intensive activities were under way in the shadow of the dormant volcano. In this decade, logging pushed into the native timber of the Toutle River area, and by 1895 a logging railroad was built in the valley. Settlement of the Lewis River, Spirit Lake Basin, and Green River Valley proceeded at a fast pace, stimulated by the possibility of profits from logging in these areas. A logging camp built at the mouth of Speelyai Creek in 1890 was supplied by the steamer *Bismark,* which sailed up the Lewis River as far as Speelyai Riffle. South of the Toutle River, logging operations near Ostrander Creek were in full swing by 1887, with eight logging camps and twenty-nine shingle mills.

In the footsteps of the loggers came miners hoping to strike it rich. On September 22, 1892, the St. Helens Mining District was organized, attracting large amounts of money into the area from numerous outside interests. Claims were staked at a rapid rate throughout areas north of Spirit Lake on into the Green River Valley. Dr. Henry Coe, owner of several claims, was most responsible for development of the area. He organized his own mining company in the late 1890s, and even sold stock to President Theodore Roosevelt.

But mining operations proved less profitable than was hoped. The amounts of extracted copper, gold, and silver did not override the high costs of trans-

Sweden Mine near Spirit Lake (This shaft is now under the lake's surface)

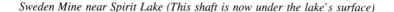

Forest Service ranger residence, Spirit Lake, circa 1930

portation and mineral refining. By 1911 most outside groups had stopped investing in mining, forcing operations to cease.

In 1897 President Cleveland consolidated all unappropriated and nonprivate lands between the Columbia River and Snoqualmie Pass into the Mount Rainier Forest Reserve, to be managed by the U.S. Department of Interior (USDI). A major private land owner was the Northern Pacific Railroad (incorporated by Burlington Northern in 1970), which held parcels of land on and adjoining Mount St. Helens. In 1908, President Roosevelt transferred control of the Mount Rainier Forest Reserve from the USDI to the U.S. Department of Agriculture (USDA) to be managed by the newly formed U.S. Forest Service. Established were the Rainier National Forest (dissolved in 1933 with the creation of Mount Rainier National Park, USDI) and the Columbia National Forest, which included Mount St. Helens. The Columbia National Forest was redesignated Gifford Pinchot National Forest in 1949 to honor the founder and first chief forester of the U.S. Forest Service.

Over the years, numerous land exchanges between Northern Pacific (Burlington) and the federal government diminished the railroad's landholdings near Mount St. Helen's, so that by 1980 Burlington owned one square mile of the volcanic summit and a few parcels of land around the mountain. With the May 18 eruption, Burlington Railroad and the federal government became co-owners of the gaping crater. On May 18, 1983, Burlington Northern donated ownership of this land, plus land near Spirit Lake, to the government for inclusion in the monument.

In 1910 the U.S. Forest Service constructed a ranger station in the town of Toutle, and built guard stations on the shores of Spirit Lake. The Forest Service increased its activities in the area by relocating the ranger station at Spirit Lake in 1913, and by building a fire lookout on the summit of Mount

Coldwater Lookout, a fire observation station until 1953

Taking Lange Road to Spirit Lake in the early 1920s

St. Helens in 1916. Attracted by the scenic beauty of Spirit Lake, private groups began to develop the area for recreational use. In 1911 the Portland YMCA received a special-use permit for a permanent campsite at the south end of the lake. In the late 1930s the YMCA purchased Dr. Coe's land at the north end of Spirit Lake and moved its establishment to that site in 1951. Spirit Lake Lodge was constructed in 1913, and by 1928 the Holmstedt Lodge, with room for fifty guests, was in operation.

Recreational use of the Mount St. Helens area continued to increase up to the first signs of volcanic activity in 1980. Although the scenery has changed, many people are enjoying and learning from the vast array of recreational and educational opportunities available at Mount St. Helens.

Euroamerican Eyewitness Accounts of Eruptions

With the completion of the 1800–1802 (T) eruptive phase, Mount St. Helens entered a period of relative quiet. But this was to be short-lived. In 1831 Mount St. Helens again showed signs of new life, sending ash and pumice over wide areas. The eruption of 1831 marked the beginning of a period of sporadic volcanic activity which was to continue until 1857.

The decade before the 1831 eruption saw increasing numbers of European and American explorers and fur traders entering areas in close proximity to Mount St. Helens, resulting in many fascinating eyewitness accounts of the volcanic activity that took place throughout the 1831–57 eruptive period.

The first authenticated eyewitness account was recorded in 1835, describing both the 1831 and 1835 eruptions. In an updated letter that appeared in the *Edinburgh New Philosophical Journal* dated January 1836, twenty-six-year-old Dr. Meredith Gairdner (1799–1837), physician for the Hudson's Bay Company at Fort Vancouver, wrote: "We have recently had an eruption of Mount Saint Helens, one of the snowy peaks of the Marine Chain on the north-west coast, about 40 miles to the north of this place (Fort Vancouver). There was no earthquake or preliminary noise here: the first thing which excited my notice was a dense haze for two or three days, accompanied with a fall of minute flocculi of ashes, which, on clearing off, disclosed the mountain destitute of its cover of everlasting snow, and furrowed deeply by what through the glass appeared to be lava streams. . . . at the same season of the year 1831, a much denser darkness occurred here, which doubtless arose from the same cause, although at that time no one thought of examining the appearance of this mountain" (Gairdner in Harris).

Paul Kane's "Mount St. Helens" (courtesy of the Royal Ontario Museum, Toronto)

An American Methodist missionary, Josiah Lamberson Parrish (1806–95), resided at the Methodist mission at Champoeg, French Prairie, about 70 miles southwest of Mount St. Helens. On November 22, 1842, he observed a sizable eruption from the mission's doorstep: "I stepped outside and noticed the eruption of Mount St. Helens, when I returned to the house and informed those inside what I had seen and they, of course, laughed the idea to scorn; but upon looking for themselves, were soon ready to admit that my assertion was correct; for upon looking at the mountain we saw arising from its summit, immense and beautiful scrolls of what seemed to be pure white steam, which rose many degrees into the heavens. Then came a stratum just below those fine huge scrolls of steam, which was an indefinite shade of gray. Then down next the mountain's top the substance emitted was black as ink" (Parrish).

One of the most fascinating accounts of eruptive activity was recalled by Peter Hardeman Burnett (1807–97), an emigrant on the Oregon trail who would later become governor of California. Vividly expressed in his letters are scenes of a large ash column rising from the mountain, which he viewed from the confluence of the Willamette and Columbia rivers: "On the sixteenth of February, 1844, being a beautiful and clear day, the mountain burned most magnificently. The dense masses of smoke rose up in one immense column, covering the whole crest of the mountain in clouds" (Burnett).

Attracted by reports of volcanic activity, Canadian artist Paul Kane (1810–71) visited the Pacific Northwest to draw water color sketches of Mount St. Helens. On March 27, 1847, he began his drawings from a vantage point at the mouth of the Lewis River, which offered a clear and unobstructed view of the mountain. Recording the event in his journal, he said: "There was not a cloud visible in the sky at the time I commenced my sketch, and not a breath of air was perceptible: suddenly a stream of white smoke shot up from the crater of the mountain, and hovered a short time over its summit; it then settled down like a cap. This shape it retained for about an hour and a-half, and then gradually disappeared" (Kane).

Developing additional sketches of Mount St. Helens from Cowlitz Farm (near the present-day town of Toledo), Kane returned to Toronto in October 1848, where he painted a composite oil on canvas which is housed at the Royal Ontario Museum, Toronto. Combining various elements from both his Lewis River and Cowlitz Farm sketches, this highly romanticized painting shows a group of Native Americans looking in awe upon the brilliance of the night eruption.

Recreational Opportunities

In August 1982 Congress sent President Reagan legislation establishing Mount St. Helens National Volcanic Monument. An area of about 110,000 acres was to be administered as a separate unit within the boundaries of Gifford Pinchot National Forest by the U.S. Forest Service. With the President's signature, much of the volcanic area became protected for present and future generations to enjoy.

Future expanded development of the National Volcanic Monument into restricted areas depends on the behavior of the volcano itself. Most likely, Mount St. Helens will continue in its present dome-building phase, with or without occasional explosive activity, and then eventually become quiet once more.

Under these circumstances, roads and trails will lead deeper into the National Volcanic Monument, expanding educational and recreational opportunities already offered. In coming years, visitors will drive to the newly formed lakes created by the debris avalanche. Access to ridge tops north of the volcano will offer views directly into the crater and its huge lava dome. Trails will weave through the volcanic landscape and will even circumvent the volcano.

Roads and trails now offer access to an amazing landscape. Future expansion of recreational facilities into restricted areas will only enhance present opportunities. Entry to the restricted zone is prohibited without a permit. Check with Monument Headquarters or Forest Service information stations on current restricted zone boundaries and new recreational opportunities available.

Road Guide

Most roads that provided access to the west and north sides of Mount St. Helens were destroyed by the May 18, 1980 eruption. Today, segments of paved and graded roads lead into the devastated zone and surrounding unaffected areas. No road crosses from east to west through the National Vol-

Mount Margaret

canic Monument. The major points of interest listed here have been separated into three sections: South Side Interpretive Sites; East/Northeast Side Interpretive Sites; and West Side Interpretive Sites. A map at the beginning of each section identifies site location and route of access. Depending on your route of travel to the National Volcanic Monument, each section or mixture of sites within individual sections will require a full day of travel. Remember, roads into the National Volcanic Monument, like most mountain roads, are often narrow, steep, and winding, requiring slow speeds and concentration on the part of the driver. Loaded logging trucks have the right of way. Stay right and use turnouts when vehicles approach you; stop or park only in areas out of traffic flow. Planning ahead on sites to be visited, gasoline stops, and other travel needs will enhance your visit to Mount St. Helens. U.S. Forest Service information specialists are on duty at Yale, Pine Creek, and Iron Creek information stations seven days a week during the summer season to answer questions.

SOUTH SIDE INTERPRETIVE SITES

Lava Casts
Elevation: 1,500 feet
Distance from crater: 7 miles
Facilities: restrooms and picnic tables

Explore the stone remnants of a forest that lived approximately 1,900 years ago. At that time, flowing rivers of pahoehoe and aa lava formed the interesting tree wells or casts we see today by surrounding standing trees and encasing them in hot lava. A natural kiln was created, producing such heat that the wood inside was reduced to charcoal. With the passing of time, remnants of the trees disappeared, leaving only vertical casts. Also seen are horizontal casts of logs that were carried along by the lava flow.

The casts are about 400 feet south of the Lava Cast Picnic Area.

Ape Cave
Elevation: 2,100 feet
Distance from crater: 6 miles
Facilities: restrooms

Hiking time: downslope about 1 hour; upslope and trail about 2.5 hours

Ape Cave is the longest known intact unitary lava tube in the continental United States, over 12,000 feet. Around 1946, Lawrence Johnson was log-

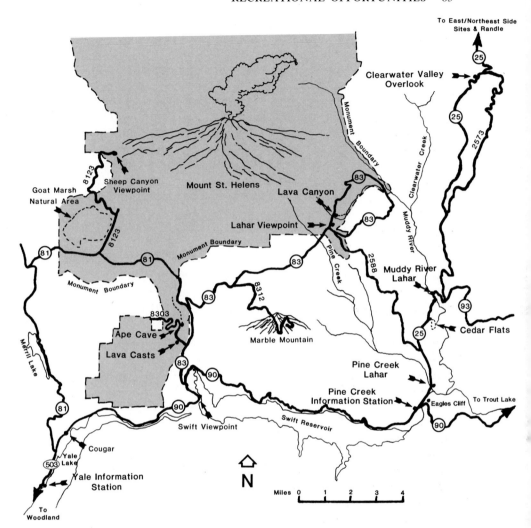

South Side Interpretive Sites

ging in the area when he noticed a tree sticking upside down, roots in the air. He went to investigate and found that the tree had fallen into the opening of a cave. Sliding down the tree, he entered the cave and explored as far as the little amount of light would allow. After he reported his discovery, a group of young outdoorsmen, named the St. Helen Apes, extensively explored the dark recesses of the cave. Ape Cave bears their name.

Mount St. Helens experienced a significant change in its eruptive behavior about 1,900 years ago. During this Castle Creek Eruptive Period, the volcano produced large flows of ropy-textured pahoehoe basalt in addition to thick dome-building dacite lava similar to that being produced today. Red-hot rivers of molten rock poured down the flanks of the volcano, killing all life as they passed over. Exposed to cool air, the surface of the lava flow crusted over, forming a hardened shell. Since lava is an excellent insulator, internal lava remained in a liquid state, flowing red hot with little loss of heat. With the end of the eruption, the liquid lava drained out downslope, leaving the tube we see today. Ape Cave and Lava Casts are part of one of these flows which extends nearly 8 miles.

Ape Cave is divided into two sections, upslope and downslope, both accessible from the main entrance. The downslope section extends about 4,000 feet, ending in a sand fill. Easily walked, this route is recommended for most visitors.

For those wishing a more rigorous experience, the upslope route offers numerous challenges. In exploring the 7,000 feet of passageway, large piles of rock debris must be crossed, narrow openings must be crawled through, and a 6-foot wall of solidified lava must be climbed. Only well-equipped explorers should attempt the upslope section. For those who do, exit to the surface can be obtained at the upper entrance, where a 1.25-mile trail leads back to the parking lot.

To make your exploration of Ape Cave safe and enjoyable, the following equipment is recommended. Each party should carry at least three sources of light A gas lantern works best, because the walls of the cave are very dark and absorb much light. Since the temperature of the cave is cool, with

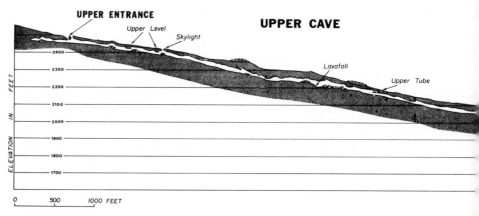

Schematic cross section of Ape Cave

Inside Ape Cave

water often dripping from the ceiling, warm, water-resistant clothes are a
must. Sturdy hiking boots are also helpful, because the lava floor is often
sharp and jagged. Gloves will protect your hands while scrambling over rocks
on the way to the upper entrance.

LOWER CAVE

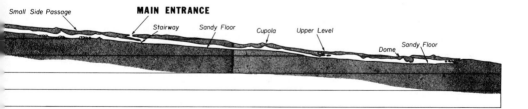

The lava level within a tube often rose and fell. Hot gases caused melting of wall surfaces, forming a dark shiny glaze. Look for pleated patterns of ripples where hot lava slumped down the tube walls.

During the melting, lava dripped from the ceiling. As the lava solidified, lava stalactites formed. Globules of lava dripping from the ceiling piled on the tube's floor, forming stalagmites. Intensive recreational use of Ape Cave has destroyed most stalagmites.

Flow marks indicate the descending order of lava level within the tube. When the lava level stabilized for a time, it congealed on the tube walls, forming flow marks much like rings on a bathtub.

Drastic drops in temperature as the lava cooled caused the walls and ceiling to contract, forming cracks. If cracking was severe, the walls and ceiling were left unsupported, allowing breakdown to occur. Today, large piles of rock litter the tube floor. Entrances sometimes form when ceiling breakdown extends to the surface. Other entrances result when no tube roof is formed. Where walls have collapsed, red soil baked by the extreme heat of the lava can be observed.

Sand, ash, and pumice are easily observed on the downslope section floor. This material has been transported into the tube by surface streams. Much of the sand found in the cave today was washed in through the lower entrance over the last 450 years.

In constricted areas, cave winds can reach velocities of 7 mph. This wind is caused by differences in air temperature inside and outside the cave. The temperature of Ape Cave remains in the mid-forties all year. Outside air temperatures fluctuate above and below cave temperature. During winter months, warm cave air rises and rushes out the upper entrance. In the summer, warmer outside air is drawn into the upper entrance as cool, dense cave air pours out of the lower entrance.

Lahar Viewpoint
Elevation: 3,000 feet
Distance from crater: 5 miles

Lahar. The destruction you see as you face the mountain occurred in a matter of minutes. At 8:32 A.M. the eruption propelled a mixture of rock, ash, and water down the eastern flank of the volcano at speeds in excess of 100 mph. Resembling an airborne avalanche, a 60-foot wall laden with logs and boulders overtopped the 120-foot section of the ridge to your right. Slowing to 60 mph, the lahar swept over your position. Splitting on the ridge directly behind you, part spilled into the steep Lava Canyon while the other portion was diverted into Pine Creek.

Upper Muddy lahar (Shoestring Glacier in background), severed at the V-notch on the crater rim

The sheer force of the lahar is evident everywhere. Stumps were battered into pulp. Most trees were removed, sheared off at ground level. Those that withstood the surging flow were gouged and splintered. Many were debarked as far up as 30 feet, with rock embedded deep within them. The lahar caused trees to whip back and forth, snapping off their tops.

Tiny "islands of survival" can be found throughout the lahar deposit. Plants were able to sprout back from soil protected behind stumps and even along the bankcuts of former roads. Colonizing plants are also seeding in, adding green to this landscape of gray.

Shoestring Glacier. The eruption removed 70 percent of the glacial ice volume on Mount St. Helens. The Shoestring Glacier, which, over thousands of years, had eroded a deep channel into the volcano's eastern flank, was severely damaged. During the first minutes of the eruption, the glacier was beheaded, as indicated by the V-notch at the crater's rim. Pyroclastic flows melted over 20 feet of snow and ice from the thickness of Shoestring Glacier, adding greatly to the size of the lahar. Lacking its sustaining ice formation, the future existence of the Shoestring Glacier is uncertain.

Lahar Stratigraphy Bands. By vertically slicing a ridge, the lahar uncovered 13,000 years of Mount St. Helens volcanic activity. Many brightly colored strata bands are layered one on top of the other, each differing in thick-

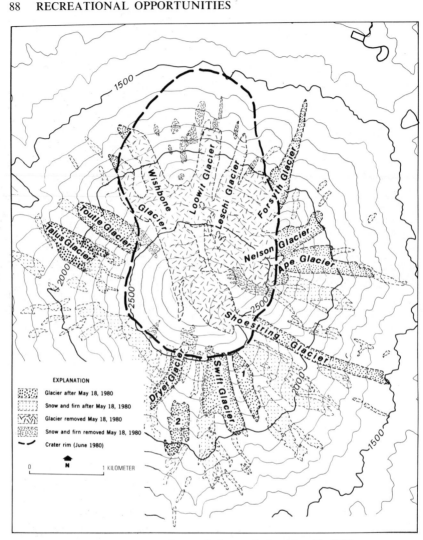

Overhead schematic of existing glaciers before and after May 18, 1980

ness and composition. Variations in bands occurred for a number of reasons. As volcanic material was deposited on the ground, it tended to stack deeper in surface depressions and shallower at high points. This explains why the bands follow an irregular course. Amounts and types of volcanic material that have covered this area have differed with each eruptive period. Before you is an open book, each band a chapter in pyroclastic flow, tephra fallout, or lahar geologic history.

Lahar stratigraphy bands

Lava Canyon
Elevation: 2,900 feet
Distance from crater: 5 miles

Before the May 18, 1980, eruption, Lava Canyon was virtually unknown, hidden from view by a dense forest canopy. As the Muddy River lahar raged down the volcano's eastern flank, a ridge split the flow, directing a portion through the narrow gorge. Trees were swept off the steep canyon walls as the gorge was scoured to bedrock. In a matter of minutes, the geologic history of over 35 million years was exposed.

Appearing as islands, large gray rock formations are found throughout most of the canyon. Deposited roughly 1,900 years ago during the Castle Creek Eruptive Period, these are about the same age as Ape Cave. At that time, a moderately fluid basalt/andesite lava flow invaded the canyon. The many amazing shapes and patterns of these formations reflect cooling processes. If lava cooled without disturbance, it contracted evenly, forming columnar joints or lava columns. More often, irregular cooling hindered column formation.

Beneath the 1,900-year-old lava flow is the yellow-colored rock of the Ohanapecosh formation. Underlying much of the Pacific Northwest region,

Muddy River cascading through Lava Canyon. Dark gray columnar formations are remnants of a lava flow of about 1,900 years ago, and light-colored rock is the Ohanapecosh formation, over 35 million years old

Mountain ridge before the birth of Mount St. Helens

Water tops ridge and erodes the predecessor to Lava Canyon

Basalt/andesite lava flow fills canyon approximately 1,900 years ago

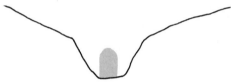

Water erodes softer Ohanapecosh formation, exposing lava ridges on canyon floor

The formation of Lava Canyon

this geologic formation is over 35 million years old. The Ohanapecosh formation is composed of lava and volcanic sediments produced by volcanoes of the ancestral Cascade Range.

The Ohanapecosh formation was uplifted and eroded into a series of mountain ridges before the birth of Mount St. Helens. Mount St. Helens began filling valleys and covering these ancestral ridges as new volcanic activity continued. When the valley filled with material, raising it to the crest of the ridge separating Mount St. Helens from Smith Creek, water began flowing over the top, eroding the ancestral formations that preceded Lava Canyon. The canyon was invaded by lava 1,900 years ago, flowing from the flanks of the volcano. Following the eruption, the Muddy River reestablished its course over the lava filling and began to erode a new canyon. The waters found the Ohanapecosh formation softer and more easily eroded than the new lava formations, leaving exposed dark ridges standing on the new canyon floor.

In places, the Muddy River waters crest these lava ridges, forming falls that plunge over 50 feet. The Muddy River has also eroded, to a lesser degree, the lava flow ridges, exposing intricate internal features.

Pine Creek Lahar
Elevation: 1,100 feet
Distance from crater: 12 miles

If you happened to be at this location on the morning of May 18, you would have witnessed an awesome sight. About thirty minutes after the initial eruption, a 30-foot wall of mud and water laden with volcanic and organic debris, traveling nearly 40 mph, crashed through this area. Stripping the banks of vegetative matter as it moved along, the flow ripped the bridge from its foundation and carried it downstream to the Lewis River. Mud lines left on surviving trees vividly illustrate how high the flow was.

The lahar generated such a great carrying capacity that it easily transported the huge boulder that is located at the south end of the new bridge next to the road. On May 19, officials found this 27-ton rock resting in the middle of the road. It took two heavy cranes to move it to its present position.

Cedar Flats Research Natural Area
Elevation: 1,300 feet
Distance from crater: 10 miles
Trail length: 1-mile loop

The 680-acre Cedar Flats Natural Area was established on March 14, 1946, to exemplify how stands of old-growth western red cedar once appeared in valley bottoms of the Cascade Range. The area's name is misleading. The major forest type in the natural area is Douglas-fir, covering 310 acres. A fire that swept through a section of this area over 125 years ago gave rise to a second-growth Douglas-fir stand which occupies 130 acres. Old-growth western red cedar, often associated with swamps and marshes, covers roughly 220 acres. Many Douglas-fir and western red cedar trees tower over 200 feet high and are over 30 feet in circumference. Interspersed with these major cover types and occupying the understory are western hemlock, Pacific silver fir, and grand fir. Hardwoods include red alder, big-leaf maple, and black cottonwood.

Thriving on the cool, moist forest floor are many aquatic and semiaquatic plant species. A mosaic of ferns, flowers, stunted trees, and conifers growing on nurse logs meets the eye.

The natural area is often used by a wide variety of wildlife, serving as a fall and winter range for Roosevelt elk and Columbian black-tailed deer. Occasional visitors are black bears, cougars, bobcats, minks, and beavers.

Cedar Flats

Muddy River Lahar
Elevation: 1,250 feet
Distance from crater: 10 miles

Shortly before 9:00 A.M., May 18, 1980, the leading edge of the Muddy River lahar reached this point. According to an eyewitness account, at about 10:00 A.M. the bridge that crossed the Muddy River had vanished and the river was "in flood." Watching the surging lahar, the viewers reported that by about 10:45 to 11:00 A.M. the flood had receded considerably but was still flowing with thick mud. Traveling nearly 15 mph, the lahar rushed into the Lewis River where it merged with the Pine Creek lahar, which had arrived about 30 minutes earlier. Together, they destroyed the Lewis River bridge and poured into Swift Reservoir.

Mud lines on trees along Muddy River (note person standing near trees at right)

Muddy River and yellow (Ohanapecosh formation) boulders

At about 5:00 P.M., yet another large lahar, composed of very different material, coursed down the Muddy River past this site. Comprising white, rounded pumice rock, ash, and fragments of wood, this lahar was generated by a pyroclastic flow that swept down the volcano's eastern flanks shortly before 4:00 P.M.

It will be years before the ravages inflicted by the Muddy River lahar will heal. The bridge that was washed out has been rebuilt; however, the destroyed bridge can still be viewed about half a mile downstream. Many of the trees toppled by the flow were sharpened to fine points. Referred to as "bayonet" trees, they aim in the direction that the lahar rushed. Riverbanks were scraped and eroded, as can be seen in the high stream bank on the other side of the road, the result of a large forested spit of land that was totally swept away. Along the margins of the lahar, many of the trees left standing died from suffocation because of the thick flow deposits over their root systems. Other trees were coated high up their trunks with mud, an indicator of the lahar's depth.

The large yellow rocks before you are found scattered for miles along the Muddy River. Carved from steep walled canyons and carried by the lahar to their present resting spot, these boulders are from the Ohanapecosh formation. Exposed to weathering processes for the first time in millions of years, they are quickly crumbling away.

Clearwater Valley Overlook
Elevation: 3,080 feet
Distance from crater: 10 miles

Ten miles east of the volcano and just outside the blast area, one can view how abruptly the destruction stopped. Standing on the fringe of green, living zone, observe the blown-down timber, standing dead timber, singed forest areas (now mostly salvaged), and living forest all in close proximity.

In 1981 the salvage of usable timber began in the Clearwater Valley. Today, most of the salvagable timber has been removed. The bulk of management activity is now focused on the reforestation of the valley. The May 18, 1980 eruption blanketed the valley with tephra fallout averaging 10 to 12

From Clearwater Valley Overlook, blown-down, standing dead, and green forest vividly illustrate the sharp edge between survival and annihilation

inches deep. Three planting crews used specially modified augers, mounted on chain-saw type engines, to drill through the nutrient-poor tephra, tapping the buried organic layer. Mixing the original soil with the tephra, crews planted a wide variety of tree seedling species so as not to create a monocultured forest. Today, Douglas-fir, western red cedar, Engelmann spruce, and cottonwoods represent the majority of seedlings covering the valley bottom. On valley walls and ridge lines, trees such as noble fir, grand fir, and lodgepole pine, which are adapted to higher elevations, have been planted. In the not too distant future, Clearwater Valley will again be green.

The Clearwater Valley is also being managed for the enhancement of wildlife habitat. Located on the valley floor, the banks of Clearwater Creek and its tributaries have been planted with hardwood saplings. These saplings serve a variety of functions. Their roots stabilize stream banks, controlling erosion. Their foliage provides shade which helps regulate stream temperature necessary for the survival of fish. They also provide food for the many deer and elk that live in the valley.

Snags are visible throughout the valley. Numbering about four per acre, they have been left intentionally to provide bird habitat. Cavity-nesting birds such as the bluebird, flicker, and hawk require a snag habitat for shelter, roosting, and nesting. Today, these and other bird species are present in the Clearwater Valley. Artificial habitat has also been provided in the form of bird boxes placed in artificially drilled holes in the snags. These highly successful boxes are used by birds as frequently as natural cavities.

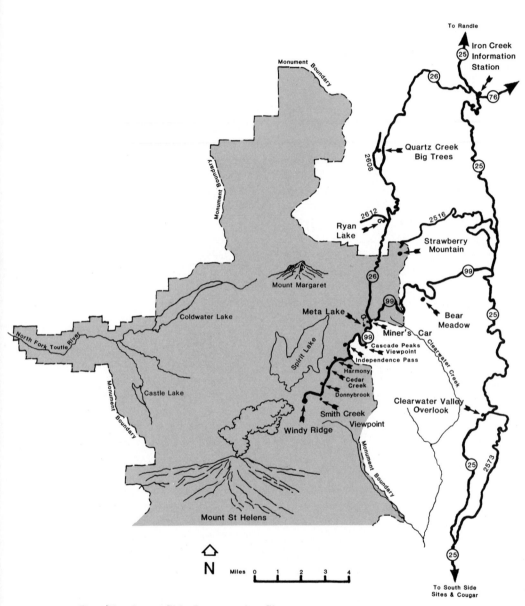

East/Northeast Side Interpretive Sites

EAST/NORTHEAST SIDE INTERPRETIVE SITES

Quartz Creek Big Trees
Elevation: 2,200 feet
Distance from crater: 15 miles
Trail length: 0.25 mile

Less than a mile from the edge of the devastated zone, this short loop trail is a must before entering the destruction. You will weave through a stand of old-growth Douglas-fir and western red cedar that tower skyward. Some of these giants are over 30 feet in circumference and 200 feet high.

With an enhanced appreciation of how forests once looked, you will easily sense the power the blast wielded on the landscape.

Ryan Lake
Elevation: 3,300 feet
Distance from crater: 12 miles

On the morning of the eruption, Ron Conner was camped on the north side of Ryan Lake. His van was parked on the east side of the small turnout on the road. Only minutes after the eruption began, the lateral blast topped the small ridge that hides the volcano from view. Conner most likely heard nothing as the blast descended on him. Timber was blown down in all directions, covering the small campground containing three picnic tables and two outhouses. Conner was found behind one of the outhouses buried under inches of volcanic and organic debris. Conner's campsite can still be viewed, with items strewn over the ground. Unfortunately, many of the items have been removed by souvenir collectors.

Parked just west of Conner's van were a pickup truck and a horse trailer. Clyde Croft and Allen Handy drove up on May 17 planning to ride to Deadman's Lake. Finding the trail still snowed in, they rode their horses about 2 miles down the road to Polar Star Mine, where they camped overnight. Handy died in his sleeping bag during the blast. The tethering ropes that secured the horses to trees had been snapped when the animals panicked as the blast enveloped them.

Croft, surviving the blast, draped his sleeping bag over himself and began to walk back to the pickup. Against all odds, he proceeded through ash that had darkened the day as he scrambled over hundreds of toppled trees.

Ryan Lake on May 11, 1980, and one year later

Reaching Ryan Lake, he drank a beer in the pickup while contemplating what to do next. The beer can was later found on top of the ash on the truck. Croft apparently decided to attempt hiking out of the blast area. With his sleeping bag over his head, he walked 5.2 miles from the truck down Road 26 before succumbing to asphyxiation. His body was later discovered by search dogs under his ash-covered sleeping bag.

Miner's Car
Elevation: 3,600 feet
Distance from crater: 9 miles

The crushed Pontiac Grand Prix is a grim reminder of the volcano's power, which took the lives of Donald, Natalie, and Richard Parker. After parking their car, they hiked about a mile to a small cabin near Black Rock Mine. As the blast topped the final ridge between the volcano and the cabin, hurricane-force winds over 200 degrees F. swept down on the Parkers, totally destroying the cabin. Only the floor remained intact, buried under 8 to 10 inches of ash and pumice.

The force of the blast lifted the car and threw it about 60 feet to the logs where it rests today. Wind-carried pumice, some of which is still embedded in the grill, sandblasted the automobile's paint.

Forest Service naturalist giving talk at site of the Parkers' crushed car

Look closely at the car. Strangely, the interior seats and door trimming melted from the extreme heat while the tires remained virtually unscathed and still filled with air. Why did this occur? One theory is that the blast rode atop a thin cushion of air as it traveled across the landscape. As superheated winds melted the interior and molding, the cooler cushion of air spared the tires. The fact that tires are made to withstand high temperatures should also be taken into consideration.

Unfortunately, the car has been heavily vandalized by souvenir hunters. To protect this cultural resource from further harm, a fence has been erected around the car.

Meta Lake
Elevation: 3,600 feet
Distance from crater: 9 miles
Trail length: 0.2 miles, paved for disabled access

Imagine a small mountain lake nestled among Pacific silver fir, noble fir, and mountain hemlock. As one walks along its cool breezy shore, numerous secluded coves are found, ideal for picnicking, fishing, or daydreaming. On a hot day, the lake's cool, clear water lures one for a swim.

Meta Lake was so described prior to May 18, 1980. But this beautiful scene was destroyed by the eruption, as ground-hugging, hurricane-force winds, deflected and funneled by contours of nearby ridges, blew down, uprooted, and snapped off trees surrounding the lake. The once lush Meta Lake area then appeared as many shades of gray, covered by ash and pumice. No visible signs of life were present immediately after the eruption.

Today, the black and white picture of the Meta Lake area is transforming into a colorful landscape. As you walk the short trail through this scene of destruction, you will notice much life that survived the eruption, such as small Pacific silver fir trees and numerous species of shrubs characteristic of mature forest understories. Covered by snow at the time of the eruption, these smaller plants survived the deadly hot gases of the blast while 150-foot-tall mountain hemlock and noble firs were toppled. By taking increment cores, scientists have determined that some of these small trees are nearly 100 years old. Shaded by mature trees which stood above them, these trees grew very slowly. Exposed to full sunlight now, they can grow more rapidly to become the future forest surrounding Meta Lake.

The trees reveal other evidence of life. Look closely at the bark. Small rodents that survived the blast in their burrows feed on the bark of these surviving trees in the absence of other vegetation. In fact, many of the trees have been killed by girdling from mammals.

Meta Lake

Many invertebrates also survived the blast. On the morning of May 18, 1980, Meta Lake was covered with a thin sheet of ice. This ice acted as a protective shield and spared the lives of most invertebrates living in the lake. Populations of brook trout are rebuilding, and Meta Lake is the first lake in the destruction zone where spawning is occurring. Salamanders that were hibernating beneath mud on the lake bottom during the blast are now thriving and multiplying.

Cascade Peaks Viewpoint
Elevation: 3,900 feet
Distance from crater: 7.5 miles

Mount St. Helens, Mount Hood, and Mount Adams are three members of a great circle of living mountains, known as the Ring of Fire, which surrounds the Pacific Ocean. These snow- and ice-covered giants, born of fire, are one of two types of mountains that make up the Cascade Range. Today's range of jagged peaks was formed when huge shifts in the earth's crust forced part of the region upward. During and following this uplift, repeated eruptions of volcanic material built towering volcanic cones on top of the new range. At the same time, the erosive action of water, wind, and ice relentlessly tore them down.

The eruption of Mount St. Helens and the resulting devastation of the surrounding landscape was not a unique event but something that has happened repeatedly to this and other Cascade volcanoes. Mount Adams, second highest peak in the Pacific Northwest at 12,286 feet, is surrounded by jagged ridges and deep, glacially incised valleys. Little is known about the eruptive history of Mount Adams. One of the most obvious characteristics of Mount Adams is its flat top. Unlike the pointed peak of Mount Hood, which was formed by eruptions through a single main vent, Mount Adams erupted material from several vents, each eruption separated by vast amounts of time. This formed Mount Adams's broad, flat summit. Notice how weather-beaten and deeply eroded its sides appear, a good indication that the volcano is very old and subject to infrequent volcanic activity.

Mount Hood, highest peak in Oregon at 11,245 feet, rises above the surrounding landscape. Violent eruptions in its past sent lava flows down its slopes and flooded ancient river canyons. Lahars appear to have reached as far as the Columbia River, 20 miles distant. As recent as the mid-19th century, eruptive activity was viewed by Native Americans and settlers, coinciding with eruptions of Mount St. Helens. Doubtless Mount Hood's past eruptions destroyed large areas of vegetation and countless wildlife. Although Mount Hood's sharp horned peak, from this vantage point, seems to indicate that it is little eroded, from other directions the volcano is highly asymmetrical. During the last glaciation, ice carved as much as 1,000 feet from Mount Hood's top and sides, transforming it from a smooth, symmetrical cone much like former Mount St. Helens to the four-faceted horn that remains today.

Ancient Mount Adams, Mount Hood in its prime, and youthful Mount St. Helens are good representatives of various stages in the cycle of volcanic growth and decline in the Cascade Range. In only a few hundred years this area will most likely again be cloaked in dense green forest. Of course, there is always the chance that Mount St. Helens or any other Cascade volcano may feel growing pains and again repeat the cycle of life and death.

Independence Pass
Elevation: 4,100 feet
Distance from crater: 7 miles
Trail length: 0.3 mile

At trail's end, Independence Pass has commanding views of Mount St. Helens, the Spirit Lake Basin, and the devastated Mount Margaret backcountry, as well as neighboring volcanoes Mount Hood and Mount Adams. The fury of the eruption is visible in all directions. Timber ripped and shattered, ''bayonet trees'' honed needle sharp, singed dead forests, and exposed con-

View from Independence Pass of June 1982 steam and ash plume

tours of the landscape stripped of vegetative cover are results of the power-
ful lateral blast. Enormous hummocky mounds of mountain debris and the
gaping horseshoe-shaped crater were created by the debris avalanche. Tephra several feet deep was deposited by the lateral blast and towering Plinian
eruption column, and fumaroles rising from the pumice plain are evidence
of still-hot buried pyroclastic flow material.

The Spirit Lake Basin is awesome. The lake is partly covered by logs
washed off surrounding ridges when the debris avalanche plunged into Spirit
Lake and forced its waters upward.

A small segment of the growing lava dome inside the crater can be seen
from Independence Pass. Before the September 1982 dome-building eruption, it was impossible to view the lava dome from Independence Pass, because it lay hidden behind the eastern crater wall. But enough lava was
extruded onto the dome's surface during that eruption to make it visible. Today, with continuing dome-building activity, more of the massive dome is
being revealed to those who visit Independence Pass.

Harmony, Cedar Creek, and Donnybrook Viewpoints
Elevation: about 4,100 feet
Distance from crater: between 5 and 6 miles

Located between Independence Pass and Smith Creek Viewpoint, each of these pullover viewpoints will whet the visitor's appetite to get closer to the volcano. Each site offers a distinctive view of Spirit Lake and Mount Margaret backcountry. Donnybrook also provides a spectacular look at the pumice plain, upper end of the debris avalanche, and Harry's Ridge.

Smith Creek Viewpoint
Elevation: 4,100 feet
Distance from crater: 4.5 miles
Facilities: picnic tables

The Upper Smith Creek Basin was severely affected by the lateral blast and consequent pyroclastic flow and lahar activity. After the blast had roared through the valley, pyroclastic flows poured down upper drainage channels, leaving deposits up to 6 feet thick. Heat produced by the blast and pyroclastic flows melted shattered glaciers and snowpack, generating a large lahar that swept down the northeastern flank of Mount St. Helens into the valley of Smith Creek. In the distance can be seen where the Smith Creek lahar merged with the Muddy River lahar.

Smith Creek Viewpoint offers a magnificent view of Mount St. Helens and surrounding ridges upon which the volcano is built. The lateral blast scoured many of the ridge faces to bedrock, giving them a multicolored appearance. Mount Adams and Mount Hood can also be seen, and on an exceptionally clear day Mount Jefferson is visible to Mount Hood's right.

Windy Ridge
Elevation: 4,000 feet
Distance from crater: 4 miles
Facilities: restrooms

Only four miles from Mount St. Helens, Windy Ridge is possibly one of the most breathtaking panoramas in the world. Geologic wonders can be seen in every direction. Mount St. Helens and its huge amphitheater crater dominate the landscape, with steam plumes occasionally rising thousands of feet above the crater rim. Two old domes, Dog's Head on the upper eastern rim and

Mount Margaret Basin and log-covered Spirit Lake from Windy Ridge

the round Sugar Bowl on the lower edge of the crater, represent formations of past eruptions which were extruded approximately 2,000 and 1,150 years ago, respectively. Mount Adams, with its slopes deeply carved by glacial ice, towers to the east.

Here, the path that the enormous debris avalanche followed as it smashed into Spirit Lake is clearly evident. Logs blown down by the blast were washed off ridges and now float on top of the lake. With your eyes, follow the ridge line on the opposite side of the lake down to the lake's surface near the hummocks of avalanche debris. This was the approximate location of Spirit Lake Lodge, managed by Harry Truman for over 50 years. "Harry's Ridge" was located directly in the path of the debris avalanche. Harry himself is presumed buried under hundreds of feet of avalanche debris and water.

On the other side of Harry's Ridge, a section of the debris avalanche ran up the slope and overtopped a 985–1,250-foot section of ridge line. Referred to as the Spillover, the avalanche continued down the other side where it affected South Coldwater Creek. In its wake were deposited large mounds of hummocky debris, often hundreds of feet thick. Similar debris can be found over a distance of 13.5 miles down the North Fork Toutle River Valley.

Nearly all the destruction viewed from Windy Ridge was caused by the lateral blast, released over the landscape when the north flank of the volcano avalanched. Windy Ridge was inundated with winds over 250 mph and temperatures of 680 degrees F. On Johnston Ridge (formerly Coldwater Ridge)

Naturalist explaining events of the eruption to monument visitors

in the distance behind Harry's Ridge, David Johnston, a USGS volcanologist, was swept to his death by the lateral blast. The exposed contours of the Mount Margaret backcountry exemplify the sheer force of the blast.

The huge pumice plain was formed as repeated pyroclastic flows, generated by explosive eruptions throughout 1980, poured from the crater's mouth and filled in the irregular topography left by the debris avalanche. Visible today are fumaroles spewing steam skyward as moisture comes in contact with hot pyroclastic material buried under the surface.

The surface elevation of Spirit Lake is about 3,460 feet, 220 feet higher than before the May 18, 1980 eruption. In fact, most of Spirit Lake seen today from Windy Ridge is new lake surface, formerly a dense old-growth forest.

Spirit Lake has been steadily increasing in size, because its natural outlet to the North Fork Toutle River was completely filled by the debris avalanche. Rain and snow melt continue to add water to the lake. Unable to drain, the surface of the lake would continue to rise unchecked and eventually overtop the unconsolidated and highly erodible debris material forming a new outlet. Studies have indicated that if this were allowed to occur, destructive mudflows could result. As a temporary solution, in November 1982 the U.S. Army Corps of Engineers began pumping water from the lake at about 85,000 gallons a minute to maintain the lake at a safe level. Lake water was pumped into a stilling basin through a 5-foot diameter, 3,400-foot-long steel pipe buried under the debris avalanche deposit. Lake water flowed into an outlet channel to the North Fork Toutle River. Without pumping, Spirit

Lake would have been about 45 feet higher and might have breeched the debris blockage. In the spring of 1984, work began on a permanent solution to the Spirit Lake problem. Scheduled for completion in April 1985, an 8,500-foot-long, 12-foot-diameter tunnel through the base of Harry's and Johnston ridges to South Coldwater Creek will keep the lake at a safe level by allowing lake water to drain by gravity down the North Fork Toutle River. Spirit Lake's surface elevation will be about 3,440 feet.

Windy Ridge is on the edge of the restricted zone. Even though the volcano may appear quiet, the possibility of avalanches, lahars, and minor debris-ejecting eruptions is very real. The size of the restricted zone will be reduced in the future as it is determined that the volcano poses less of a danger.

Bear Meadow
Elevation: 4,000 feet
Distance from crater: 11 miles
Facilities: restrooms and picnic tables

On the morning of May 18, 1980, several parties were camped at Bear Meadow, one of the best sites to view Mount St. Helens, hoping to see the volcano in action. Little did they realize how much action they would witness.

Among those camped were Gary Rosenquist, an amateur photographer, and Keith Ronnholm, a graduate student in geophysics. Early that morning, Rosenquist had placed his camera on a tripod. When he realized that the north flank of the volcano was avalanching, he captured through his lens a remarkable sequence of eruption photographs, showing the beginning of the debris avalanche and the killing blast cloud it released. Aware that the cloud was rapidly approaching his position, he snapped a few last pictures while members of his party began to warn other campers who were unaware of the impending disaster. Then Rosenquist rushed to his vehicle and raced down Road 99 to safety.

Ronnholm was relaxing in his camper those first moments of the avalanche. Hearing people yelling outside, he peered from his window to see what was causing the commotion. Seeing the north side of the volcano avalanching, he grabbed his camera and rushed outside to take pictures. Not realizing the magnitude of the eruption, and expecting the cloud to be diverted upward by ridges closer to the volcano, Ronnholm remained at his original campsite photographing the dark blast cloud, which now completely hid the mountain. The ground-hugging cloud kept coming, topping one ridge after another. After about 40 seconds had elapsed, Ronnholm fully realized

Series of pictures taken of May 18 eruption from Bear Meadow and Road 99

his peril and ran to his car in hopes of outdistancing the cloud. Stopping about 3 miles down Road 99, he pulled over and began to photograph the cloud, which was rising above his position. Lightning arced between portions of the eruption cloud, and thunder was a continuous rumble. Rocks the size of golf balls began to fall around him, so he again fled in his car. In seconds, ash the consistency of wet mud began to fall from the sky, sticking to his windshield. The ash rapidly changed to the texture of light dust, and was so thick that he could see only a few feet in any direction. Unable to follow the ash-covered road, he parked and waited, wondering what would happen next. He noticed a red glow in his rearview mirror quickly approaching. To his relief, the glow was caused by the headlights of a logging truck, also trying to escape. By following the logging truck, which was directed by two men who walked in front feeling for the sides of the road with their feet, Ronnholm escaped to the north and safety.

Today, how close those camped at Bear Meadow came to death is vividly apparent. Situated on ridge tops less that 0.5 mile away are seared trees, testimony to the killing heat of the blast. Slightly farther in the distance, with the volcano and its gaping crater as a backdrop, are ridges where trees were blown down. Ronnholm was indeed correct; the blast cloud was diverted upward by a ridge, the last ridge before Bear Meadow.

Strawberry Mountain Viewpoint
Elevation: 5,200 feet
Distance from crater: 10 miles
Trail length: 0.5 mile

Strawberry Mountain offers some of the best auto access views of Mount St. Helens available. You can look directly into the gaping crater and see the steaming lava dome growing inside. Look at the volcano and imagine the north flank avalanching directly toward you, releasing the lateral blast cloud over the landscape. As it rushes toward your position, the cloud tops all land forms, sweeps over the Mount Margaret high country, and plunges into the Green River drainage directly in front of you. All forests are destroyed in its path. Within seconds, it ascends up Strawberry Mountain, leaving trees singed and dead.

A trail, which begins 1 mile before the viewpoint on Road 2516, leads to the top of Strawberry Mountain and commanding views in all directions. Mount Adams, Mount Rainier, Mount Hood, and Mount St. Helens dominate the landscape, with the enormous blast area vividly contrasted against the green forest.

WEST SIDE INTERPRETIVE SITES

Debris Dam Overlook
Elevation: 1,100 feet
Distance from crater: 14 miles

For those who don't have time to spend a full day exploring Mount St. Helens National Volcanic Monument, Debris Dam Overlook (about 6 miles west of the monument) offers an excellent opportunity to view some dramatic effects of the eruption. From I-5, drive 27.5 miles east on Highway 504 to the Debris Dam Overlook.

Castle Lake, formed when the debris avalanche dammed Castle Creek

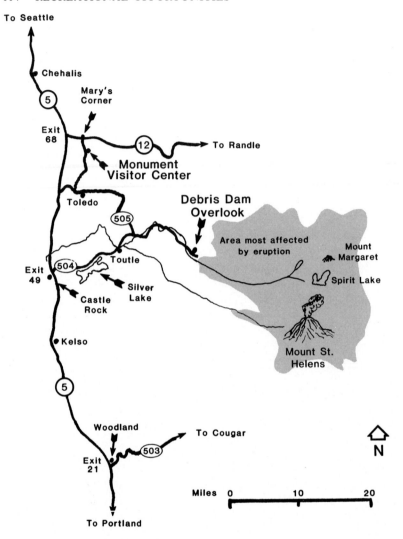

West Side Interpretive Sites

You are standing at the toe end of one of the largest landslides in recorded history. The huge debris avalanche, 0.65 cubic mile of rock, snow, and ice, coursed down the North Fork Toutle River Valley traveling 13.5 miles in 10 minutes. Ascend a small hillside and gaze at rocky mud flats, distant ridge lines barren of timber, and Mount St. Helens.

Engineers determined that the debris avalanche, composed of unconsolidated, highly erodible material, posed a serious threat to down-river communities. Hundreds of thousands of tons of sediment were being washed from the debris avalanche and transported down the valley to the Cowlitz River, causing serious flood hazards. In an attempt to control this situation, the U.S. Army Corps of Engineers had, by November 1980, constructed a debris-retaining structure at the end of the avalanche flow. It was 6,100 feet long (two sections) and 43 feet high and had the sediment-retaining capacity of 6 million cubic yards.

The Debris Dam has been breached several times since its completion, usually during severe rainstorms, and also by the March 19, 1982 eruption, which sent a lahar down the North Fork Toutle River. Damage to the dam has been repaired, and it continues to prevent millions of cubic yards of material from moving downstream.

Another effect of the avalanche was that with the valley plugged with debris, small tributaries that flowed into the North Fork Toutle River were blocked. As water backfilled tributary valleys, new ponds and lakes were created in the unstable terrain. Coldwater and Castle lakes, nonexistent before the eruption, are located about 10 miles upriver from the Debris Dam Overlook. Down-river communities were again faced with flash-flood hazards, since these lakes could eventually overtop and breach the debris blockage. To stabilize these lake surface levels, the Corps of Engineers constructed permanent revetment outlet channels for Coldwater and Castle lakes.

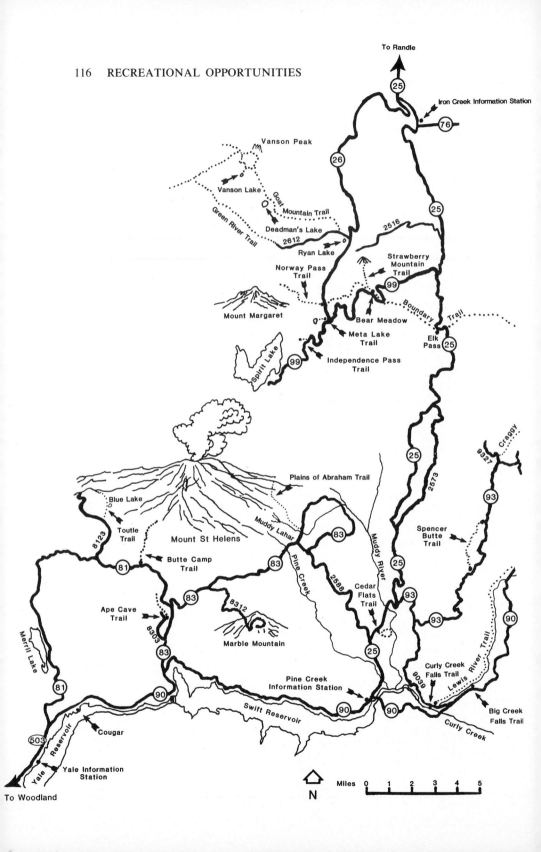

Trail Guide

Like roads, most trails that lead through the backcountry near Mount St. Helens were destroyed during the blast. But trails outside devastated areas remained intact, though they were often covered by inches of volcanic fallout. Old trails are being reconstructed and new ones planned and built both inside and outside monument boundaries, offering many miles of scenic enjoyment.

The travel season for trails is, of course, dependent on the weather. Lower-elevation trails usually open by mid-May, but in high country above 4,000 feet, trails are seldom free of snow until early to mid-July. For all except the experienced winter hiker, the hiking season usually draws to a close by late-October to mid-November, when the first heavy snows fall.

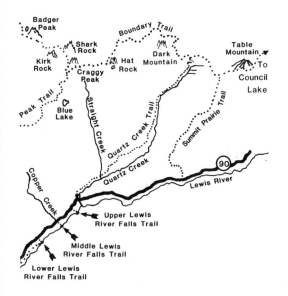

Yale, Pine Creek, and Iron Creek information stations, the Monument Visitor Center, or the National Volcanic Monument Headquarters at Amboy can supply up-to-date information on trail openings and closures, conditions, areas of restricted entry, new trail opportunities, access routes, and the type of use allowed on the trail. Topographic maps detailing Mount St. Helens before the eruption can also be helpful, since many of the trails still exist or have been reconstructed at their original locations. (See trail map on these pages.) Again, check with Forest Service information personnel.

Hiking into the devastated zone can be grueling and dangerous. Downed trees are often unstable and covered with loose bark. Thin coverings of ash and pumice provide a slippery surface for walking. If you follow a trail, please stay on it. Taking shortcuts can cause personal injury as well as unsightly damage to open areas. Since vegetative cover was removed by the blast, hiking can be made miserable by rain, wind, and sun. Use common sense before setting out, and be sure to pack adequate water, food, and clothing and travel at a reasonable pace. Be alert for signs identifying the restricted zone.

No backcountry permits are required for overnight camping within the National Volcanic Monument (except in restricted-entry areas) or the surrounding Gifford Pinchot National Forest. When camping in the devastated zone, use only camp stoves for fire and protect the volcanic area for others to enjoy. And no matter where you camp, try to leave behind no traces of your presence.

Some trails listed have been discussed in the Road Guide section. Please refer to that section for trail description.

At this time no mountain climbing is allowed on Mount St. Helens because of the restricted zone. Fortunately, in close proximity are Mount Rainier National Park, Mount Hood National Forest, and the Mount Adams and Goat Rocks wilderness areas, which offer mountain and rock climbing challenges for both the beginner and the expert. If you plan to camp overnight, wilderness permits are required from June 15 to November 15 at Mount Adams and Goat Rocks wilderness areas and year-round at Mount Rainier National Park.

Permits are free and may be obtained in person or by writing National Park or Forest Service headquarters or individual ranger district offices. Since all regulations may change, alway check for current information.

Toutle Trail No. 238

Length: 2.5 miles, one way	Hiking time: 4 hours, round trip
High point: 3,550 feet	Difficulty: moderate
Elevation gain in: 350 feet	Use season: July through October
Elevation gain out: 650 feet	Restrictions: no ORV use

The first 0.1 mile of the Toutle Trail is somewhat difficult to follow, owing to repeated washouts. Find and cross the stream using the small temporary log bridge. From this point the trail is in fairly good shape.

At 0.2 mile the trail skirts beautiful Blue Lake. This lake was formed several hundred years ago when a lahar blocked a stream, causing its waters to back up. In recent years Blue Lake has increased in size because of beaver activity. The trail continues through an impressive stand of noble fir and an open understory. At approximately the 1 mile point, the trail enters an old clearcut, allowing a commanding view of the volcano, only 3 miles distant. On the opposite side of the clearcut the trail again enters forest and descends to Sheep Canyon. The effects of the May 18 eruption are everywhere. This drainage channel was scoured to bedrock as a lahar roared off the volcano, removing all life in its path. Notice how the lahar banked on slopes as it followed the course of the drainage. Towering waterfalls are visible, cascading 75 feet to deep pools. In the distance, the South Fork Toutle River Valley can be seen, lined with blown-down trees that were flattened by the lateral blast. The Toutle Trail once led to the South Fork Toutle River but was partly removed during the eruption, so access is now difficult.

From the Road 503/81 junction, 0.5 miles west of Cougar, drive 13 miles on Road 81 to Road 8123. Proceed 1.7 miles on Road 8123 to where the road forks. Take the right fork 0.1 mile to the signed trailhead. The Toutle Trail may also be accessed by driving about 1.5 miles past the Butte Camp trailhead (see Butte Camp Trail description) on Road 81 to the Road 81/8123 junction. Follow Road 8123 as explained above.

The Toutle Trail is now under contract to be restored, so before beginning your hike you should check with a monument information station for possible route changes.

Wash marks formed when a lahar swashed back and forth as it roared down Sheep Canyon

Butte Camp Trail No. 238A

Length: 2 miles, one way, to Butte Camp; 2.7 miles to timberline

High point: 4,500 feet

Elevation gain: 1,400 feet

Hiking time: 4 hours, round trip

Difficulty: difficult

Use season: June through October

Restrictions: hiking only

Butte Camp Trail is an exciting trek up the southern slopes of Mount St. Helens. You will begin by crossing open lava beds which flowed down the volcano's slopes almost 2,000 years ago. After about 0.5 mile, the trail becomes difficult to locate. Follow the old road cut to your left and keep bearing right. In about 0.3 mile a sign will mark where the Butte Camp Trail continues. The trail steepens as it winds through lodgepole pine. Breaking into an open subalpine forest, it then proceeds on a high ridge toward the lofty mass of Mount St. Helens. At 2 miles (elevation 4,000 feet) the trail forks. To the left is a small meadow area known as Butte Camp. The right fork climbs steeply for 0.7 mile to timberline. The panorama is magnificent, with views of Mount St. Helens and Mount Hood.

From Road 90 take Road 83 to the Road 83/81 junction (3 miles). On Road 81 proceed 3 miles to the signed trailhead.

Ancient lava flow along Butte Camp Trail

Ape Cave Trail No. 239

Length: 1.25 miles, one way
Hiking time: 1 hour, round trip
Difficulty: easy

Use season: April through October
Restrictions: hiking only

Used as a return route from the upper entrance of Ape Cave, this trail offers stunning views of Mount St. Helens. Stroll through surface deposits of 2,000-year-old lava flows. Look for the ropy textured pahoehoe lava. In about 0.2 mile, the trail winds through a dead forest, smothered by an alluvial outwash which swept down the volcano's slopes in 1980. Sand and sediments continue to build in this area. For those with time and equipment, try the loop through the upper end of Ape Cave, returning via the Ape Cave Trail (see Ape Cave description). Remember: Take nothing but pictures; leave nothing but footprints; kill nothing but time.

From Road 90 take Road 83 to Road 8303 (1.8 miles). Turn left and proceed 1 mile to Ape Cave.

Plains of Abraham Trail No. 234

Length: 2.7 miles
High point: 4,400 feet
Elevation gain: 1,400 feet
Difficulty: difficult

Hiking time: 5 hours
Use season: July through October
Restrictions: no ORV use

The Plains of Abraham Trail is one of the most exciting hikes in the monument. You will view a landscape devastated by a lahar, walk through cool, green forest, and relax at meadows of pumice spotted with wildflowers, huckleberries, and alpine trees. All this is possible, along with breathtaking views of Mount St. Helens and surrounding volcanoes.

You will begin by winding through a forest along the northern edge of the Muddy River lahar. Imagine those first few minutes of the eruption as the lahar raced down the slopes of Mount St. Helens and thundered past your position. At about 0.5 mile the trail begins to climb and skirts a ridge that was topped and scoured by the lahar. Continuing to climb, the trail meanders in and out of tall stands of mountain hemlock and Douglas-fir, with glimpses of Mount St. Helens looming in the background. At about 2 miles you will enter a semiopen subalpine area and follow a ridge dotted with pockets of trees killed by the blast, living forest, and meadows covered with wildflowers. At 2.5 miles leave the forest and gape down the notch of Ape Canyon, formed over thousands of years as water cut through the rock wall. At 2.7 miles the trail terminates at the Plains of Abraham, a 0.5-mile-wide and almost level area void of nearly all forms of life. Before the eruption, the

Plains of Abraham was kept free of trees by huge avalanches which swept off the upper slopes of Mount St. Helens. On May 18, 1980, a huge lahar, formed when the blast melted ice and snow, rolled through this area and poured through Ape Canyon. Later that day, pumice rained from the sky giving the Plains of Abraham the appearance of a moonscape.

The Plains of Abraham Trail is scheduled to be extended to Windy Ridge in the near future, so check with Forest Service information personnel about its possible extension. The trailhead is 0.2 mile north of the lahar interpretive site on Road 83. Make sure to bring plenty of water.

Cedar Flats Trail
Length: 1-mile loop   Use season: year-round
High point: 1,300 feet   Restrictions: hiking only
Difficulty: easy

This trail penetrates a cool forest of old-growth western red cedar and Douglas-fir. See the Road Guide section for a full description.

Spencer Butte Trail No. 30
Length: 3.2 miles, one way   Difficulty: moderate
High point: 4,247 feet   Use season: June through October
Elevation gain: 850 feet   Restrictions: none
Hiking time: 3 hours, round trip

Offering fantastic views of towering volcanic peaks and rock bluffs, the Spencer Butte Trail is a popular destination for hikers of all ages. Wander through open meadows created when the Spencer Butte burn swept through this area in the 1920s. Wildflowers and huckleberries abound, adding color and fragrance to the landscape. As you reach the summit, investigate the remnants of an old fire lookout. The lookout is a particularly fine place to sit and view Mount St. Helens, Mount Adams, Mount Rainier, Mount Hood, and Mount Jefferson while eating lunch.

Drive north 1 mile on Road 25 past the Muddy River viewpoint. At the junction of Road 25 and Road 93, proceed on Road 93 for 8 miles. On your left you'll notice a signed trailhead for Spencer Butte. This route is 1.7 miles to the summit, mostly through forest. An alternate route is to drive 3 miles farther on Road 93 to a second signed trailhead. This trail is 1.5 miles to the summit through sparse forest and open meadows.

Craggy Peak Trail No. 3

Length: 4.5 miles, one way
High point: 5,200 feet
Elevation gain: 1,600 feet
Hiking time: 5 hours, round trip

Difficulty: moderate
Use season: mid-July through
October
Restrictions: none

The trail meanders for a mile through a forest of Douglas-fir, western hemlock, and Pacific silver fir and then enters a clearcut area. On the far side of the cut, the trail enters a beautiful forested meadow area. Lush grass carpets the forest floor. As the trail continues to climb through a sub-alpine environment, ridge after ridge of solid forest can be observed in the foreground of majestic Mount Adams. At about 3 miles you enter the Shark Rock Scenic Area, where Blue Lake (elevation 4,553 feet) glistens below. An unmarked trail leads down to the lake shore. From meadows bursting with wildflowers, view Mount Rainier, Mount Adams, Shark Rock, Kirk Rock, Hat Rock, and

Ape Canyon

Snagtooth Mountain. The trail terminates just south of Craggy Peak, where it joins the Boundary Trail.

To reach the trailhead, drive 3 miles past the second Spencer Butte trailhead on Road 93 (see Spencer Butte description) to Road 9327. Turn left on Road 9327 and proceed 0.5 mile to Road 040. Turn right and follow 040 about a mile to the trailhead.

Curly Creek Falls Trail No. 31B

Length: 0.3 mile
Use season: March through
  November

Restrictions: no ORV use;
  not recommended for horse travel

Follow the trail as it steeply descends through a lush conifer forest to the Lewis River. On the opposite side, water descends 75 feet from Curly Creek. The erosive power of the water has carved a natural arch and is now in the process of forming a second.

The Curly Creek trailhead is on the opposite side of the road from the Lewis River trailhead on Road 9039.

Big Creek Falls Trail No. 31C

Length: 0.1 mile
Use season: March through
  November

Restrictions: no ORV use;
  not recommended for horse travel

Walk downstream 0.1 mile along the rim of a steep gorge. Behold the breathtaking panorama of Big Creek Falls as it plunges 125 feet into an amphitheater-shaped canyon. Take extreme care along the canyon rim.

Drive 9 miles on Road 90 past the Road 25/90 junction to the Big Creek bridge and pull-off area.

Lewis River Trail No. 31 and Lower Lewis River Falls

Length: 11 miles, one way
High point: 1,600 feet
Elevation gain: about 400 feet
Hiking time: day hike (one way)
  or overnight

Difficulty: easy
Use season: March through
  November
Restrictions: no ORV use

This trail provides miles of easy roaming through a cool, green forest along a semiremote segment of the Lewis River. Follow gentle ups and downs while

Curly Creek Falls

paralleling the Lewis River on its northern bank for about 2.7 miles to Bolt Camp shelter, built in the early 1930s. Many hikers stop at this campsite for an overnight stay. At about 4 miles the trail leaves the river and climbs up the north side of the canyon. Large old-growth firs and cedars serve as a canopy of green. The forest floor is carpeted with Oregon grape, deerfoot vanilla leaf, and waist-high vegetation. The old-growth trees soon give way to a young forest, resulting from the Spencer Butte fire. Far below, the Lewis River slowly cuts through the canyon floor. At about 8.5 miles the trail gradually descends to the Lewis River near Cussed Hollow Creek. In this area, look for stumps that have been cut or chiseled out. These cut marks are called springboard holes because loggers from days past inserted springboards to stand on while cutting the tree. Crossing the bridge over Cussed Hollow Creek, the trail travels a short distance to Crab Creek and Road 90. People experienced in rafting often float from Crab Creek to Swift Reservoir. Crossing Road 90, the Lewis River Trail continues 1.2 miles to the Lower Lewis River Falls and campground. The falls are breathtaking. Over 100 feet wide, uniform cascades of water fall 40 feet to a deep pool. It is often remarked that these falls are a miniature Niagara Falls. Good fishing awaits those who bushwack down to the plunge pool. The Lower Falls are also easily accessible from the Lower Falls campground.

The Lewis River Trail is an excellent one-way hike and is possible when a vehicle is left at each trail terminus. From the Road 25/90 junction, drive 5.2 miles up Road 90 to unpaved Road 9039. Turn left and proceed 1 mile to a large sign identifying the Lewis River Trail. The second car can be left 9 miles farther north on Road 90 at the Lewis River campground.

Lower Lewis River Falls

Middle Lewis River Falls Trail No. 31E

Length: 0.6 mile, one way

Difficulty: moderate

Use season: March through
November

Restrictions: no ORV use;
not recommended for horse travel

Few trails of such short distance and ease of travel offer so much beauty. Proceeding through a lush, green forest, you come to Copper Creek and rustic Copper Creek Bridge. A short distance after crossing the bridge you will view Copper Creek Falls cascading 40 feet. The trail continues on a steeper grade to the Middle Falls of the Lewis River. Bring a picnic lunch and try your luck at fishing below the falls.

The trailhead is on Road 90 one mile past the Lower Lewis River Falls campground.

Upper Lewis River Falls Trail No. 31F

Length: 0.3 mile, one way

Difficulty: moderate

Use season: March through
November

Restrictions: no ORV use;
not recommended for horse travel

As you steeply descend through the conifer forest, the roar of the falls grows ever louder. At the end of the trail, Alec Creek joins the Lewis River. The falls are breathtaking, forming a horseshoe-shaped amphitheater over 100 feet wide and 40 feet high. Excellent fishing exists below the falls.

The trailhead starts off of Road 90 two miles past the Lower Lewis River Falls campground.

Quartz Creek Trail No. 5

Length: 10.5 miles, one way

High point: 4,200 feet

Elevation gain: 2,400 feet

Hiking time: overnight

Difficulty: difficult

Use season: July through October

Restrictions: no ORV use;
not recommended for horse travel

What makes Quartz Creek such a memorable hike is the remoteness of the area. Not heavily used, Quartz Creek Trail is an excellent choice for the hiker who wants to get away from it all. The Quartz Creek Valley is one of the few remaining areas yet to experience any logging activity. Numerous creeks parallel and crisscross the trail, most without bridges. Be prepared to ford these waters. For the first 2 miles, the trail winds through forest to Platinum Creek and then climbs above the Quartz until it again drops to a small campsite near the confluence of Straight and Quartz creeks. When crossing the log over Straight Creek, walk upstream 200 feet to a beautiful series of cascading waterfalls. About 100 feet downstream is another waterfall at the confluence of Straight Creek and Quartz Creek. The trail continues through forest for the majority of its remaining length, passing Snagtooth Creek at 4 miles, and on into the Upper Quartz Creek drainage. At approximately 8 miles the trail enters an old burn area on Dark Mountain before terminating on a ridge top at the junction with the Boundary Trail.

The signed trailhead is on Road 90 by the Quartz Creek Bridge, 17 miles from the 25/90 junction.

Summit Prairie Trail No. 2

Length: 9 miles, one way, from
  Road 90; 7 miles, one way, from
  Road 9075
High point: 5,238 feet

Elevation gain: 2,650 feet
Difficulty: difficult
Use season: July through October
Restrictions: none

For those desiring panoramic views of towering mountain peaks and uncut forested ridges and valleys, Summit Prairie Trail is an excellent choice. The trailhead leaves from Road 90 and climbs steeply through forest for 2 miles and then intersects Road 9075. The trail continues in forest with a steep grade for about 3 more miles and then rewards the hiker's efforts with easy ridge walking and outstanding views of the surrounding countryside. The trail meanders for 4 miles on a ridge top through semiopen forest and subalpine meadows. On either side of the ridge line are uncut Quartz Creek and French Creek valleys, with Mount Adams, Mount Rainier, and Mount St. Helens looming in the distance. Near the junction with the Boundary Trail explore the remnants of the old Summit Prairie lookout. If you have the time and energy, connect with the Quartz Creek Trail and complete the multiday loop through these impressive valleys.

The Summit Prairie trailhead is 22.5 miles from the 25/90 junction on Road 90. For those who wish to shorten the hike, the first 2 miles can be eliminated by beginning from a trailhead located on Road 9075. Drive 15.5 miles on Road 90, turn left on Road 9075, and proceed 5.5 miles to where the road forks. Turn right and go 0.5 mile to the signed trailhead.

Mount Rainier from summit of Strawberry Mountain

Strawberry Mountain Trail No. 220

Length: 2.5 miles, one way
High point: 5,464 feet
Elevation gain: 1,500 feet
Difficulty: moderate

Use season: mid-July through
   October
Restrictions: hiking only

Climb steeply through a dense conifer forest. Tantalizing glimpses of Mount Adams and the surrounding countryside spur the hiker on. At about 2 miles the trail leaves the green forest and follows a ridge top, the edge of the blast zone. Mount St. Helens and the growing lava dome inside its crater dominate the landscape. At the summit, the hike is climaxed by magnificent views in all directions. Stare over endless valleys and ridges to Mount Adams, Mount Hood, and Mount Rainier. In the direction of Mount St. Helens, the full scope of the destructive force of the eruption is realized. You are literally standing on the edge of life and death, where the destruction stopped at the summit upon which you stand. Take time for a picnic lunch and look for wild strawberries, especially delicious because water is scarce.

The Strawberry Mountain trailhead starts directly across Road 99 from Bear Meadow. A 0.5-mile trail to the summit of Strawberry Mountain begins at the 6-mile point on Road 2516.

Meta Lake Trail

Length: 0.2 mile, one way
High point: 3,600 feet
Difficulty: easy (paved for
    disabled access)

Use season: late-June through
    October
Restrictions: hiking only

Walk to Meta Lake through a forest leveled by the blast. Yet life survived. See the Road Guide section for a full description.

Independence Pass Trail No. 227

Length: 0.3 mile, one way
High point: 4,100 feet
Difficulty: easy

Use season: July through October
Restrictions: hiking only

Stunning views of Mount St. Helens and the Spirit Lake Basin reward the hiker of this trail. See the Road Guide section for a full description.

Norway Pass Trail (Section of Boundary Trail No. 1)

Length: about 2.2 miles, one way
High point: 4,508 feet
Elevation gain: 1,000 feet
Hiking time: 4 hours

Difficulty: moderate
Use season: July through October
Restrictions: hiking only

No other hike can match these views of devastated areas in Mount St. Helens National Volcanic Monument. Look down to Spirit Lake and out to Mount St. Helens and its lava dome. Look west to the rugged ridges of the Mount Margaret backcountry, where green is again returning. Look east to glacially carved Mount Adams, a backdrop to endless green valleys and ridge lines. From the parking lot, hike through the blast area, where trees have been blown down in all directions. At about 1 mile the trail steepens, climbing to a ridge top and Norway Pass. The views are incredible. Spirit Lake is huge, partly covered by logs that were washed from surrounding ridges by waves over 800 feet high. On the far end of the lake, notice the huge pumice plain created by the enormous debris avalanche and pyroclastic flows. Standing 9 miles from Mount St. Helens, look directly into the gaping crater and view the huge steaming dacite dome.

To reach the trailhead, proceed 1 mile north on Road 26 from the Road 99/26 junction. The Norway Pass Trail is scheduled to be lengthened to Mount Margaret, so check with Forest Service information personnel on its status.

Goat Mountain Trail No. 217

Length: 9 miles, one way	Difficulty: difficult
High point: 5,600 feet	Use season: July through October
Elevation gain: 2,300 feet	Restrictions: no ORV use
Hiking time: overnight	

The first 0.7 mile of the Goat Mountain Trail was buried under blown-down timber during the eruption. The area has now been salvage logged, and the trail is scheduled for reconstruction and possible relocation. Before attempting to hike the Goat Mountain Trail, check with Forest Service information personnel about the trail's status.

The trail climbs steeply for 1.6 miles, first through a salvage logged area and then a lush, green fir and hemlock forest. Reaching the open ridge, 4,600 feet, the trail becomes the dividing line between life and death. To the south, destruction caused by the eruption is awesome, actually stopping where you stand. In places, the blast spilled over onto the north slope of the ridge, leaving singed dead trees. Stare directly into the crater of Mount St. Helens and view the growing lava dome. To the north and east, Mount Rainier and Mount Adams appear as white jewels compared with the darker form of Mount St. Helens. The trail continues to skirt the ridge in a semiopen subalpine environment and at 2 miles passes above a spring-fed lakelet. Huckleberries and wildflowers abound, and views of the surrounding landscape are breathtaking. At 3.7 miles the trail passes above two more lakelets and begins to descend 900 feet down the north side of the ridge through mountain hemlock and Pacific silver fir to Deadman's Lake, at 5.5 miles, an excellent spot to camp, fish, and swim. The trail continues from Deadman's Lake and climbs 1 mile to a ridge and more commanding views of the countryside. After about 1.5 miles of ridge walking, you will come to a junction, elevation 4,700 feet. One-half mile to the right on trail No. 217A is Vanson Peak and tremendous views in every direction. Following trail No. 217B one-quarter mile to the left, a short, steep spur trail leads to Vanson Lake and excellent fishing. See both Vanson Peak and Vanson Lake by completing the 2.6-mile loop trail. Hikers with more time may want to continue on to the Green River Trail (see description) and complete a 19-mile loop. Make sure to leave cars at both trailheads, since they are 4.2 miles apart.

The Goat Mountain trailhead is 0.1 mile past the Ryan Lake interpretive site on Road 2612.

View from Norway Pass of Mount St. Helens and Spirit Lake Basin before and after May 18, 1980

Green River Trail No. 213

Length: 7 miles, one way   Difficulty: moderate
Elevation loss in: 600 feet   Use season: March through
Elevation gain out: 600 feet   November
Hiking time: 10 hours or overnight   Restrictions: no ORV use

The beginning 0.5 mile of the Green River Trail is buried under blown-down timber and is scheduled for reconstruction and possible relocation. Make sure to check with Forest Service information personnel about the trail's status before starting your hike.

From the end of Road 034 bushwack about 0.5 mile through blown-down timber, always staying parallel to the Green River, which runs to your left. When you begin to enter green forest, bear left toward the river until you intersect the trail. For the next 6.5 miles meander on gentle ups and downs while paralleling the Green River. Old-growth fir and cedar dominate the forest, their full crowns providing a nearly solid canopy, which shields the forest floor from sunlight. Along the full length of the trail are excellent opportunities for camping and fishing. Keep a lookout for evidence of old mining activity, but please don't collect souvenirs.

At 7 miles the Green River Trail No. 213 joins with Goat Mountain Trail No. 217. For the more adventuresome, the secluded Green River Falls can be found by continuing straight at the junction on No. 213 for about 200 yards and then bushwacking left down to the river, always listening for the falls. One can return via the Green River Trail or turn right on No. 217 and hike an often steep 3.2 miles to the trail junction for Vanson Peak and Vanson Lake (see Goat Mountain Trail description). From here continue the 9 miles of the Goat Mountain Trail to near Ryan Lake. Have a car at both trailheads if you intend to do the Green River/Goat Mountain trail loop.

To reach the Green River Trail, take Road 2612 for 2.5 miles past Ryan Lake to where spur Road 034 branches right just before the Green River Bridge. Continue on Road 034 for 1.7 miles to its end.

Boundary Trail No. 1

Length: about 35 miles, one way   Use season: July through October
High point: 5,100 feet   Restrictions: none except within the
Elevation gain: about 4,700 feet   National Volcanic Monument,
Hiking time: backpack   west of Bear Meadow,
Difficulty: difficult   where hiking only is allowed

This is a ridge journey which extended from Council Lake, in the shadow of 12,286-foot Mount Adams, to Spirit Lake, prior to the eruption. Although

Dark Meadow and Mount Adams from Boundary Trail

Gasoline: None available in the monument. Gas stations at Amboy, Castle Rock, Cougar, Eagles Cliff, Longview/Kelso, Morton, Packwood, Randle, Silver Lake, Toledo, Toutle, Vancouver, Woodland.

Groceries and ice: Same locations as for gasoline. Numerous independent convenience stores dot roadways leading to the monument.

Laundry: Self-service laundry at Cougar and Randle.

Medical services: Hospitals at Morton and Vancouver; Emergency Medical Teams on duty at Pine Creek Work Center (during the summer) and Randle. Medical emergency telephone number, 911.

Post Office: Amboy, Castle Rock, Cougar, Morton, Packwood, Randle, Woodland.

Telephones: Beaver Bay, Cougar, Saddle Dam, and Yale campgrounds. Communities of Cougar and Randle. Emergency telephone at Pine Creek Information Station.

Towing: Cougar Union Station, Randle Shell Station, and AAA Automobile Club of Washington State.

Campgrounds and Picnic Areas

Many public and private campgrounds are near the volcano. Information on private campgrounds can be obtained by asking locally or writing in advance to local chambers of commerce. Campgrounds in the following list range from highly developed to primitive. Facilities available at individual campgrounds are listed. Small camping fees may be requested. Use the key below to get in touch with individual administrators of campgrounds for further information. *Key:* (C) County; (DNR) Department of Natural Resources; (DPU) Department of Public Utilities, City of Tacoma; (NF) National Forest; (PPL) Puget Power and Light; (SP) State Parks.

RV Parks

Numerous recreational vehicle parks are located along I-5 and Highways 12 and 503. Consult city chambers of commerce or inquire locally for locations.

Naturalist Services

The Mount St. Helens National Volcanic Monument Visitor Center operates year-round. Drive 2 miles east off I-5 on Highway 12, Exit 68, turn right at Mary's Corner and proceed 1.5 miles to the center. It provides a compre-

Name	▲	⛺	🚐	⛽	⚡	🚻	📞	🍽	🚶	🎣	⛵	♿	$
Battleground Lake (SP) 2 mi north of Battleground	50	57		*	*	*	*	*	*	*	*	*	*
Bear Meadow (NF) 5 mi west on Road 99 from Road 99/Road 25 junction		3			*	*							
Beaver Bay (PPL) 2 mi east of Cougar on Road 90	63	5		*	*	*	*	*	*	*	*		*
Blue Lake Creek (NF) 14.2 mi south of Randle on Road 23	12				*	*			*				
Cougar Camp and Park (PPL) 0.5 mi east of Cougar on Road 90	45	15			*	*	*	*	*	*	*		*
Eagle Cliff (PPL) 1 mi east of Pine Creek Info. Station on Road 90	10				*	*		*	*	*			

Name	▲	帀	🚐	📷	🔌	🛏	🎧	🍴	🚶	🎣	⛷	♿	💲
Glenoma Park (C) 0.5 mi SW off HWY 12 Glenoma Road					*	*		*					
Ike Kinswa (SP) 20 mi east off I-5 on HWY 12	103	50	40	*	*	*	*	*	*	*	*	*	*
Iron Creek (NF) 9.7 mi south of Randle on Road 25	105	3			*	*		*					*
La WisWis (NF) 7 mi east of Packwood on HWY 12	100	6			*	*		*				*	*
Lava Casts (NF) 1.5 mi north of Road 90 on Road 83. Turn left on Road 8303 for 0.5 mi		5				*							
Lewis and Clark (SP) 3 mi east off I-5 on HWY 12—Exit 68. Turn right at Mary's Corner, travel 1 mi	25	52			*	*	*	*	*			*	*

	(1)	(2)	(3)										
Lower Lewis River Falls (NF) 14 mi east of Pine Creek Info. Station on Road 90	26								*	*			
Mayfield Lake Park (C) 25 mi east off I-5 on HWY 12	61	50		*	*	*	*	*	*	*	*	*	*
Merrill Lake (DNR) 6 mi north of Cougar on Road 81	7	5			*	*		*	*	*	*		
Merwin Park (PPL) 10 mi east of Woodland on HWY 503		135		*	*	*	*	*	*	*	*	*	*
Mossy Rock Park (DPU) 18 mi east off I-5 on HWY 12. Enter Mossy Rock and follow signs	60	50	22	*	*	*	*	*	*	*	*	*	*
North Fork (NF) 11.8 mi south of Randle on Road 23	33				*	*			*	*			*
Paradise Point (SP) 4 mi south of Woodland on I-5	79	20		*	*	*	*	*	*	*	*	*	*

Name	▲	🏕	🚐	🚽	🚻	☎	⛵	🚶	🏊	🎣	♿	💲
Saddle Dam (PPL) 4 mi east of HWY 503/Road 90 junction	14	10	*	*	*	*	*	*	*	*		*
Seaquest (SP) 5 mi east of Castle Rock on HWY 504	70	100	16		*	*	*					*
Speelyai Park (PPL) 20 mi east of Woodland on HWY 503		25		*	*		*	*	*	*		
Swift (PPL) 18 mi east of Cougar on Road 90	93	16	*	*	*	*	*	*	*	*		*
Tower Rock (NF) 8.5 mi south of Randle on Road 23. Turn on Road 28, travel 1 mi to Road 76, 1.5 mi to camp	22			*	*		*			*		*
Yale Park (PPL) 2 mi west of Cougar on Road 90		30	*	*	*		*	*	*	*		

hensive view of the May 18 eruption and resulting geologic changes through films, exhibits, and photographs. Forest Service interpretive naturalists are available to answer questions about the volcano. A pay telephone, vault toilet, water, and disabled facilities are available. A new visitor center will soon be under construction next to Silver Lake within Seaquest State Park on Highway 504 and is expected to be in operation by 1986.

During the summer months, Forest Service interpretive naturalists conduct walks, talks, and hikes at sites throughout the monument. Campfire programs are also held at various campgrounds on weekend evenings. Contact the National Volcanic Monument Headquarters, National Volcanic Monument Visitor Center, Yale, Pine Creek, and Iron Creek information stations, or look for posted interpretive program schedules for times and locations of activities.

Fishing

The eruption of Mount St. Helens severely affected many surrounding lakes, rivers, and streams. As a result, many of these waters have been closed or limited for fishing. Contact Forest Service information personnel about which areas are open for fishing. However, most waterways outside the National Volcanic Monument and devastated areas still offer excellent fishing without newly imposed restrictions. With fishing regulations continually changing, it is recommended that you consult a Washington State Fishing Rules and Regulations pamphlet for complete information. Pamphlets are provided by the Department of Fisheries (salmon) and the Department of Game (trout, steelhead, whitefish, bass, and perch). (See the Sources of Information section for addresses.)

Anyone sixteen or older needs a Washington State fishing license. For salmon, a punch card and salmon stamp must also be obtained. Licenses may be obtained at most stores in the area.

Hunting

State and federal lands surrounding Mount St. Helens are open for hunting, except the restricted zone, which is closed to all entry without a permit. A state hunting license is required regardless of age; a supplemental game stamp is required to hunt deer, elk, bear, and cougar. For complete rules and regulations, and for exact dates of hunting seasons, consult the Hunting Seasons and Rules pamphlet or contact the State Department of Game. (See the Sources of Information section for addresses.)

Weather

Weather conditions vary greatly between the west and east sides of the Cascade Range. On and near Mount St. Helens, the average annual precipitation is 90 to 120 inches with increasingly less moisture the farther one travels eastward. Winter temperatures seldom dip below zero, and summer maximums are usually in the 80s.

Mid-June through October are the best months to tour the monument. Summer days are customarily hot and dry with mild evening temperatures. Beginning in late fall, rain increases through the winter: a typical day is wet and overcast. Snow is usually found above 4,000 feet, closing many roads into the monument. Rain continues into spring, often accompanied by wind.

Sources of Information

Chambers of Commerce: Chehalis 98532; Kelso 98626; Longview 98632; Morton 98356; Vancouver 98600; Woodland 98674

Kelso Volcano Center: Exhibits tell the story of the May 18, 1980, eruption. Open 9-5 daily during the summer. Small admission fee.

Woodland Tourist Information Center: Open 8–6, closed Wednesday and Thursday.

Gifford Pinchot National Forest (NF): Up-to-date list of interpretive and visitor services, permits, new areas open, road conditions and closures, maps. Headquarters: 500 West 12th Street, Vancouver, WA 98660

National Volcanic Monument: Amboy, WA 98601

Randle Ranger District: Randle, WA 98377

Packwood Ranger District: Packwood, WA 98361

Wind River Ranger District: Carson, WA 98610

Mount Rainier National Park: Tahoma Woods, Star Route, Ashford, WA 98304

State Department of Natural Resources (DNR) (campsites, permits) (main office): Public Land Building, Olympia, WA 98504

State Department of Fisheries (main office): 115 General Administration Building, Olympia, WA 98504

State Department of Game (main office): 600 North Capitol Way, Olympia, WA 98504

Washington State Parks (SP) (main office): 7150 Clearwater Lane, KY-11, Olympia, WA 98504

Pacific Power and Light (PPL), Recreation Facilities Department: 920 SW 6th, Portland, OR 97204

City of Tacoma, Department of Public Utilities (DPU), Community Media Services: P.O. Box 11007, Tacoma, WA 98411

Lewis County (C), Parks and Recreation Department: P.O. Box 297, Chehalis, WA 98532

Appendix 1.
Glossary of Volcanic and Related Terms

Aa. Hawaiian word used to describe a lava flow whose surface is broken into rough angular fragments.

Active volcano. A volcano that is erupting. Also, a volcano that has erupted within historical time and is considered likely to do so again (there is no distinction between "active" and "dormant" in this sense).

Andesite. Volcanic rock (or lava) usually very fine grained and medium in color and containing 54 to 63 percent silica and moderate amounts of iron and magnesium.

Ash. Fine pyroclastic material fragments less than one-tenth inch in diameter. Ash in this sense is quite distinct from ash produced by common combustion, because the rocks do not catch fire and burn during a volcanic event.

Ash flow. An avalanche of hot volcanic ash and gases.

Avalanche. A large mass of material or mixtures of material falling or sliding rapidly under the force of gravity. Avalanches are often classified by their content, such as snow, ice, soil, or rock. A mixture of these materials is a debris avalanche.

Basalt. Volcanic rock (or lava) that usually is dark in color, contains 45 to 54 percent silica, and generally is rich in iron and magnesium.

Bomb. Fragment of molten or semimolten rock 2.5 inches to many feet in diameter which is blown out during an eruption. Because of their plastic condition, bombs are often modified in shape during their flight or by impact.

Caldera. The Spanish word for cauldron, a large basin-shaped volcanic depression—by definition at least a mile in diameter. Such large depressions are typically formed by the subsidence of volcanoes. Crater Lake occupies the best-known caldera in the Cascades.

Cinder cone. A volcanic cone formed by the accumulation of volcanic ash or cinders around the vent.

Glossary compiled from Foxworthy and Hill 1982, MacDonald 1972, McKee 1976, Harris 1980, Decker and Decker 1981.

Conduit. The feeding pipe of a volcano, the "throat" through which material passes on its way to the earth's surface. When filled with congealed lava (a plug), a central conduit is often relatively resistant to erosion. As a result, the solidified conduit fill-ins can remain standing as high pinnacles after the surrounding cone has been eroded away.

Continental plate. Thick crust underlying a continent.

Crater. A steep-sided, usually circular depression formed by either explosion or collapse of a volcanic vent.

Dacite. Volcanic rock (or lava) that usually is very fine grained or glassy and light in color and contains 63 to 69 percent silica and moderate amounts of sodium and potassium.

Debris avalanche. A rapid and usually sudden sliding or flowing of unsorted masses of rock and other material. In the eruption of Mount St. Helens, it was a rapid mass movement that included fragmented cold and hot volcanic rock, water, snow, glacier ice, trees, and some hot pyroclastic material. Most of the May 18 deposits in the upper valley of the North Fork Toutle River and in the vicinity of Spirit Lake are from the debris avalanche.

Dike. Relatively thin walls of solidified lava which cut through, vertically and obliquely, the interior of a volcanic cone. Dikes are formed when liquid lava rises to fill cracks or crevices within the volcano.

Dome. A steep-sided mass of viscous (doughy) lava extruded from a volcanic vent, often circular in formation and spiny, rounded, or flat on top. Its surface is often rough and blocky as a result of fragmentation of the cooler, outer crust during growth of the dome.

Dormant volcano. Literally "sleeping." A volcano that is not erupting but is considered likely to erupt in the future.

Ejecta.. Material thrown out by a volcano, including pyroclastic material (tephra) and, from some volcanoes, lava bombs.

Era. A geologic time unit of the highest order, comprising more than one period.

Eruption. The process by which solid, liquid, and gaseous materials are ejected onto the earth's surface by volcanic activity. Eruptions range from quiet overflow of liquid rock to the violent expulsion of pyroclastics.

Erosion. Processes whereby rock material is loosened or dissolved and removed from any part of the earth's surface.

Extinct volcano. A volcano that is not erupting and is not likely to do so for a long time in the future.

Fault. A crack or fracture in the earth's surface. It may represent the juncture between two adjoining blocks or plates into which the earth's crust is broken. Movement along the fault can cause earthquakes or, in the process of mountain building, can release underlying magma and permit it to rise to the surface.

Fauna. The animals of any place or time that live in association with each other.

Fissure. Elongated fractures or cracks on the slopes of a volcano or any ground surface. Fissure eruptions typically produce liquid flows, but pyroclastics may also be ejected.

Flora. The plants of any place or time that live in association with each other.

Fumarole. An opening at the earth's surface from which water vapor and other gases are emitted, often at high temperature.

Glacier. A flowing mass of ice.

Harmonic Tremor. A continuous release of seismic energy typically associated with the underground movement of magma. It contrasts distinctly with the sudden release and rapid decrease of seismic energy associated with the more common type of earthquake caused by slippage along a fault.

Holocene epoch. The 10,000- to 12,000-year-long period since the end of the Pleistocene Epoch (Ice Age). It is the present geologic period.

Lahar. A torrential flow of water-saturated volcanic debris down the slope of a volcano in response to gravity. A type of mudflow.

Lapilli. Literally, "little stones." Round to angular rock fragments measuring one-tenth to 2.5 inches in diameter. They may be ejected in either a solid or molten state.

Lava. General term for magma molten rock that has been erupted onto the surface of the earth.

Lava flow. An outpouring of lava onto the land surface from a vent or fissure. Also, a solidified tonguelike or sheetlike body formed by outpouring lava.

Lava tubes. Caves or tubes formed inside a lava flow. Although there are several means by which lava caves can be created, the most common explanation is that the liquid interior of a lava stream continues to flow after the top and sides have cooled and hardened. The center of the flow then drains away, leaving behind a hollow tube. The solidified crust of the flow forms the sides and roof of the tunnel.

Magma. Molten rock beneath the surface of the earth.

Magma chamber. The subterranean cavity containing the gas-rich liquid magma that feeds a volcano.

Magnitude. A numerical expression of the amount of energy released by an earthquake, determined by measuring earthquake waves on standardized recording instruments (seismographs). The number scale for magnitudes is logarithmic rather than arithmetic; therefore, deflections on a seismograph for a magnitude 5 earthquake, for example, are ten times greater than those for a magnitude 4 earthquake, 100 times greater for a magnitude 3 earthquake, and so on.

Mudflow. A flow of debris lubricated with a large amount of water.

Pahoehoe. Hawaiian word for congealed lava that is characterized by a smooth, ropy, or billowy surface. It is contrasted to aa, which has a rough, slaggy crust. Pahoehoe flows often contain lava tubes or caves, such as Ape Cave.

Phreatic explosion. An explosive volcanic eruption caused when water and heated volcanic rocks interact to produce a violent expulsion of stream and pulverized rocks. Magma is not involved.

Plate tectonics. The theory that the earth's crust is broken into about a dozen large plates which slowly move.

Pleistocene epoch. Period of geologic time immediately preceding the Holocene Epoch and lasting from 2 or 3 million to 10,000 years before the present. It was characterized by repeated development of ice caps and valley glaciers in the Cascade Range, hence is popularly known as the Ice Age. Most of the large composite volcanoes in the Cascades were erected during this period.

Plinian cloud. The column of gases, ash, and larger rock fragments rising from the crater or other vent. If it is of sufficient volume and velocity, this gaseous column may reach many miles into the stratosphere, where high winds will carry it long distances.

Pliocene epoch. Period of geologic time immediately preceding the Pleistocene and lasting from about 10 to 2 or 3 million years before the present. During this epoch, numerous shield volcanoes and basaltic cones were built in the Cascades.

Pumice. Light-colored, frothy volcanic rock usually of dacite or rhyolite composition, formed by the expansion of gas in erupting lava.

Pyroclastic. Pertaining to fragmented rock material formed by a volcanic explosion or ejection from a volcanic vent.

Pyroclastic flow. Lateral flowage of a turbulent mixture of hot gases and unsorted pyroclastic material (volcanic fragments, crystals, ash, pumice, and glass shards) that can move at high speed (50 to 100 miles an hour). The term can also refer to the deposit so formed.

Quaternary period. The geologic period that includes both the Pleistocene and Holocene epochs. It began a maximum of 3 million years ago.

Rhyolite. Volcanic rock (or lava) usually light in color, containing 69 percent silica or more, and rich in potassium and sodium.

Ring of Fire. The region of mountain-building earthquakes and volcanoes surrounding the Pacific Ocean.

Shield volcano. A broad, gently sloping volcanic cone.

Silica. A chemical combination of silicon and oxygen.

Subduction. A process involving the thrusting of oceanic crust beneath the margin of the continent.

Subduction zone. The zone of convergence of two tectonic plates, one of which usually overrides the other.

Tephra. Materials of all types and sizes that are erupted from a crater or volcanic vent and deposited from the air.

Vent. An opening at the earth's surface from which volcanic materials are erupted.

Viscosity. A measure of the resistance of a fluid to flow.

Volcano. A vent in the earth's crust from which volcanic products issue, or a mountain that has been built up by the eruptive products from a vent.

Weathering. The disintegration and decomposition of rock exposed to the atmosphere.

Appendix 2. Conversion Tables

Linear Measure

1 mile = 5,280 feet
1 foot = 12 inches
1 kilometer = 1,000 meters
1 meter = 100 centimeters

English-Metric Conversions

1 inch = 2.54 centimeters
1 foot = 0.3048 meter
1 yard = 0.9144 meter
1 mile = 1.609 kilometers
1 acre = 0.4047 hectare
1 square mile = 2.590 square kilometers
1 cubic mile = 4.168 cubic kilometers

Metric-English Conversions

1 centimeter = 0.394 inch
1 meter = 3.281 feet
1 kilometer = 0.6214 mile
1 hectare = 2.471 acres
1 square kilometer = 0.386 square mile
1 cubic kilometer = 0.240 cubic mile

Temperature Scales

0 degree C. = 32 degrees F.
100 degrees C. = 212 degrees F.
Formula to change Fahrenheit to Celsius: $C = \dfrac{F-32}{1.8}$

Formula to change Celsius to Fahrenheit: $F = (C \times 1.8) + 32$

Appendix 3. Geologic Time Scale

Era	Period	Epoch	Approximate Age before Present (millions of years)
Cenozoic	Quaternary	Holocene (recent)	0.015
		Pleistocene	2–3
	Tertiary	Pliocene	10–13
		Miocene	25
		Oligocene	36–40
		Eocene	58–60
		Paleocene	63–70
Mesozoic	Cretaceous		135
	Jurassic		180
	Triassic		225–230
Paleozoic	Permian		270–280
	Pennsylvanian		310–325
	Mississippian		340–350
	Devonian		400
	Silurian		430–440
	Ordovician		500
	Cambrian		570–600
Precambrian			3,500 +

Data from McKee 1976 and Bullard 1976.

Appendix 4. Plants

Following is a list of plants found at Mount St. Helens National Volcanic Monument and surrounding Gifford Pinchot National Forest.

Conifers

Douglas-fir *Pseudotsuga menziesii*
Engelmann spruce *Picea engelmannii*
Grand fir *Abies grandis*
Lodgepole pine *Pinus contorta*
Mountain hemlock *Tsuga mertensiana*
Noble fir *Abies procera*

Pacific silver fir *Abies amabilis*
Subalpine fir *Abies lasiocarpa*
Western hemlock *Tsuga heterophylla*
Western red cedar *Thuja plicata*
Western white pine *Pinus monticola*
Whitebark pine *Pinus albicaulis*

Broadleaf Trees

Big-leaf maple *Acer macrophyllum*
Black cottonwood *Populus trichocarpa*
Red alder *Alnus rubra*
Red-osier dogwood *Cornus stolonifera*

Rocky Mountain maple *Acer glabrum*
Vine maple *Acer circinatum*
Willows *Salix* sp

Shrubs

American devil's club *Oplopanax horridum*
Bearberry (Kinnikinnick) *Arctostaphylos uva-ursi*
Common juniper *Juniperus communis*
Mountain huckleberry *Vaccinium membranaceum*
Oceanspray *Holodiscus discolor*
Oregon boxwood *Pachistima myrsinites*
Oregon grape *Berberis nervosa*
Oval-leaf huckleberry *Vaccinium ovalifolium*

Pacific blackberry *Rubus ursinus*
Pacific mountain ash *Sorbus sitchensis*
Prickly currant *Ribes lacustre*
Red-flowering currant *Ribes sanguineum*
Red huckleberry *Vaccinium parvifolium*
Red mountain heath *Phyllodoce empetriformis*
Salal *Gaultheria shallon*
Salmonberry *Rubus spectabilis*
Sitka alder *Alnus sinuata*
Stink currant *Ribes bracteosum*
Willows *Salix* sp.

Herbs (flowers)

Alaska fringecup *Tellima grandiflora*
Alpine Willowweed *Epilobium alpinum*
Alumroot *Heuchera* sp.
Arrowleaf groundsel *Senecio triangularis*
Asters *Aster* sp.
Avalanche lily *Erythronium montanum*
Bear grass *Xerophyllum tenax*
Broadleaf lupine *Lupinus latifolius*
Bunchberry dogwood *Cornus canadensis*
Burnet *Sanguisorba* sp.
Buttercup *Ranunculus* sp.
Cinquefoil *Potentilla* sp.
Cliff penstemon *Penstemon rupicola*
Columbia lily *Lilium columbianum*
Columbia monkshood *Aconitum columbianum*
Coolwort foamflower *Tiarella unifoliata*
Common camas *Camassia quamash*
Common monkeyflower *Mimulus guttatus*
Cow-parsnip *Heracleum lanatum*
Cutleaf goldthread *Coptis laciniata*
Deerfoot vanilla leaf *Achlys triphylla*
Dwarf bramble *Rubus lasiococcus*
European strawberry *Fragaria vesca*
False bugbane *Trautvetteria carolinensis*
False lily of the valley *Maianthemum dilatatum*
Field horsetail *Equisetum arvense*
Fireweed *Epilobium angustifolium*
Foxglove *Digitalis purpurea*
Grass-of-Parnassus (Rocky Mountain parnassia) *Parnassia fimbriata*
Great hedge nettle *Stachys cooleyae*
Indian Paintbrush *Castilleja* sp.
Larkspur *Delphinium* sp.
Littleflower penstemon *Penstemon procerus*

Menzies silene (Catchfly) *Silene menziesii*
Mountain wallflower *Erysimum torulosum*
Northern inside-out flower *Vancouveria hexandra*
Oarleaf eriogonum *Eriogonum pyrolaefolium*
Oregon oxalis *Oxalis oregana*
Pacific bleedingheart *Dicentra formosa*
Pacific lupine *Lupinus lepidus*
Partridge foot *Luetkea pectinata*
Pearly everlasting *Anaphalis margaritacea*
Pioneer violet *Viola glabella*
Prince's pine (Pipsissewa) *Chimaphila umbellata*
Queencup (Beadlily) *Clintonia uniflora*
Red baneberry *Actaea rubra*
Rockcress *Arabis* sp.
Saxifrage *Saxifraga* sp.
Scarlet painted cup *Castilleja miniata*
Scouler corydalis *Corydalis scouleri*
Sedges *Carex* sp.
Sierra Boykinia *Boykinia major*
Sitka columbine *Aquilegia formosa*
Skunk cabbage *Lysichitum americanum*
Smelowskia *Smelowskia ovalis*
Spirea *Spirea* sp.
Stonecrop *Sedum* sp.
Sundew *Drosera* sp.
Sylvan goatsbeard *Aruncus sylvester*
Thistle *Cirsium* sp.
Trefoil foamflower *Tiarella trifoliata*
Trillium *Trillium ovatum*
Twinflower marsh marigold *Caltha biflora*
Western thimbleberry *Rubus parviflorus*
Youth-on-age (Piggyback plant) *Tolmiea menziesii*

Ferns

Bracken fern *Pteridium aquilinum*
Deer fern *Blechnum spicant*
Lady fern *Athyrium filix-femina*
Licorice fern *Polypodium glycyrrhiza*

Maidenhair fern *Adiantum pedatum*
Oak fern *Gymnocarpium dryopteris*
Parsley fern *Cryptogramma crispa*
Sword fern *Polystichum munitum*

Appendix 5. Wildlife

Following is a list of wildlife found at Mount St. Helens National Volcanic Monument and surrounding Gifford Pinchot National Forest.

Mammals

Badger *Taxidea taxus*
Big brown bat *Eptesicus fuscus*
Black bear *Ursus americanus*
Black rat *Rattus rattus*
Bobcat *Lynx rufus*
Brush rabbit *Sylvilagus bachmani*
Bushy-tailed woodrat *Neotoma cinerea*
California ground squirrel *Citellus beecheyi*
California myotis *Myotis californicus*
California red-backed vole *Clethrionomys occidentalis*
Chickaree *Tamiasciurus douglasi*
Columbian black-tailed deer *Odocoileus hemionus columbianus*
Cougar *Felis concolor*
Coyote *Canis latrans*
Deer mouse *Peromyscus maniculatus*
Dusky shrew *Sorex obscurus*
Eastern cottontail *Sylvilagus floridanus*
Ermine *Mustela erminea*
Fisher *Martes pennanti*
Fringed myotis *Myotis thysanodes*
Giant pocket gopher *Thomomys bulbivorus*
Golden-mantled squirrel *Citellus saturatus*
Heather vole *Phenacomys intermedius*
Hoary bat *Lasiurus cinereus*
Hoary marmot *Marmota caligata*

House mouse *Mus musculus*
Keen myotis *Myotis keenii*
Least chipmunk *Eutamias minimus*
Little brown myotis *Myotis lucifugus*
Long-eared myotis *Myotis evotis*
Long-legged myotis *Myotis volans*
Long-tailed vole *Microtus longicaudus*
Long-tailed weasel *Mustela frenata*
Marten *Martes americana*
Masked shrew *Sorex cinereus*
Mazama pocket gopher *Thomomys mazama*
Mink *Mustela vison*
Mountain beaver *Aplodontia rufa*
Muskrat *Ondatra zibethica*
Northern flying squirrel *Glaucomys sabrinus*
Northern pocket gopher *Thomomys talpoides*
Northern water shrew *Sorex palustris*
Norway rat *Rattus norvegicus*
Opossum *Didelphis virginiana*
Oregon vole *Microtus oregoni*
Pacific jumping mouse *Zapus trinotatus*
Pacific mole *Scapanus orarius*
Pacific water shrew *Sorex bendirei*
Pika *Ochotona princeps*
Porcupine *Erethizon dorsatum*
Racoon *Procyon lotor*
Red fox *Vulpes fulva*

Richardson vole *Microtus richardsoni*
River otter *Lutra canadensis*
Roosevelt elk *Cervus canadensis*
Snowshoe hare *Lepus americanus*
Short-tailed weasel *Mustela erminea*
Shrew-mole *Neurotrichus gibbsi*
Silver-haired bat *Lasionycteris noctivagans*
Striped skunk *Mephitis mephitis*
Townsend big-eared bat *Plecotus townsendi*
Townsend chipmunk *Eutamias townsendi*

Townsend mole *Scapanus townsendi*
Townsend vole *Microtus townsendi*
Trowbridge shrew *Sorex trowbridgei*
Vagrant shrew *Sorex vagrans*
Western gray squirrel *Sciurus griseus*
Western pipistrel *Pipistrellus hesperus*
Western spotted skunk *Spilogale gracilis*
White-tailed jackrabbit *Lepus townsendii*
Yellow-bellied marmot *Marmota flaviventris*
Yellow pine chipmunk *Eutamias amoenus*
Yuma myotis *Myotis yumanensis*

Birds

American bittern *Botaurus lentiginosus*
American coot *Fulica americana*
American goldfinch *Spinus tristis*
American kestrel *Falco sparverius*
American redstart *Setophaga ruticilla*
American robin *Turdus migratorius*
American widgeon *Anas americana*
Anna's hummingbird *Calypte anna*
Bald eagle *Haliaeetus leucocephalus*
Band-tailed pigeon *Columba fasciata*
Bank swallow *Riparia riparia*
Barn swallow *Hirundo rustica*
Barred owl *Strix varia*
Belted kingfisher *Megaceryle alcyon*
Bewick's wren *Thryomanes bewickii*
Black-backed three-toed woodpecker *Picoides arcticus*
Black-billed magpie *Pica pica*
Black-capped chickadee *Parus atricapillus*
Black-chinned hummingbird *Archilochus alexandri*
Black-headed grosbeak *Pheucticus melanocephalus*
Black rosy finch *Leucosticte atrata*
Black swift *Cypseloides niger*

Black tern *Chlidonias niger*
Black-throated gray warbler *Dendroica nigrescens*
Blue grouse *Dendragapus obscurus*
Blue-winged teal *Anas discors*
Bohemian waxwing *Bombycilla garrula*
Brewer's blackbird *Euphagus cyanocephalus*
Brown creeper *Certhia familiaris*
Brown-headed cowbird *Molothrus ater*
Bufflehead *Bucephala albeola*
Bushtit *Psaltriparus minimus*
Calliope hummingbird *Stellula calliope*
Canada goose *Branta canadensis*
Cedar waxwing *Bombycilla cedrorum*
Chestnut-backed chickadee *Parus rufescens*
Chipping sparrow *Spizella passerina*
Chukar *Alectoris chukar*
Cinnamon teal *Anas cyanoptera*
Cliff swallow *Petrochelidon pyrrhonota*
Common crow *Corvus brachyrhynchos*
Common flicker *Colaptes auratus*
Common goldeneye *Bucephala clangula*
Common loon *Gavia immer*
Common merganser *Mergus merganser*

Common nighthawk *Chordeiles minor*
Common raven *Corvus corax*
Common redpoll *Acanthis flammea*
Common snipe *Capella gallinago*
Cooper's hawk *Accipiter cooperii*
Dark-eyed junco *Junco hyemalis*
Dipper *Cinclus mexicanus*
Downy woodpecker *Picoides pubescens*
Dusky flycatcher *Empidonax oberholseri*
Evening grosbeak *Hesperiphona
    vespertina*
Ferruginous hawk *Buteo regalis*
Flammulated owl *Otus flammeolus*
Fox sparrow *Passerella iliaca*
Gadwall *Anas strepera*
Golden eagle *Aquila chrysaetos*
Golden-crowned kinglet *Regulus
    satrapa*
Golden-crowned sparrow *Zonotrichia
    atricapilla*
Goshawk *Accipiter gentilis*
Gray-crowned rosy finch *Leucosticte
    tephrocotis*
Gray jay *Perisoreus canadensis*
Great blue heron *Ardea herodias*
Great gray owl *Strix nebulosa*
Great horned owl *Bubo virginianus*
Greater yellowlegs *Totanus
    melanoleucus*
Green-winged teal *Anas crecca*
Hairy woodpecker *Picoides villosus*
Hammond's flycatcher *Empidonax
    hammondii*
Harlequin duck *Histrionicus histrionicus*
Hermit thrush *Hylocichla guttata*
Hermit warbler *Dendroica occidentalis*
Herring gull *Larus argentatus*
Hooded merganser *Lophodytes
    cucullatus*
Horned lark *Eremophila alpestris*
House finch *Carpodacus mexicanus*
House sparrow *Passer domesticus*

House wren *Troglodytes aedon*
Killdeer *Charadrius vociferus*
Lazuli bunting *Passerina amoena*
Lewis' woodpecker *Asyndesmus lewis*
Lincoln's sparrow *Melospiza lincolnii*
Loggerhead shrike *Lanius ludovicianus*
Long-billed dowitcher *Limnodromus
    scolopaceus*
Long-billed marsh wren *Telmatodytes
    palustris*
Long-eared owl *Asio otus*
Macgillivray's warbler *Oporornis tolmiei*
Mallard *Anas platyrhynchos*
Mountain bluebird *Sialia currucoides*
Mountain chickadee *Parus gambeli*
Mountain quail *Oreortyx pictus*
Mourning dove *Zenaidura macroura*
Myrtle warbler *Dendroica coronata*
Nashville warbler *Vermivora ruficapilla*
Northern shrike *Lanius excubitor*
Northern-three-toed woodpecker
    Picoides tridactylus
Olive-sided flycatcher *Nuttallornis
    borealis*
Orange-crowned warbler *Vermivora
    celata*
Osprey *Pandion haliaetus*
Peregrine falcon *Falco peregrinus*
Pied-billed grebe *Podilymbus podiceps*
Pileated woodpecker *Dryocopus pileatus*
Pine grosbeak *Pinicola enucleator*
Pine siskin *Spinus pinus*
Pintail *Anas acuta*
Poor-Will *Phalaenoptilus nuttallii*
Prairie falcon *Falco mexicanus*
Purple finch *Carpodacus purpureus*
Pygmy nuthatch *Sitta pygmaea*
Pygmy owl *Glaucidium gnoma*
Red-breasted nuthatch *Sitta canadensis*
Red crossbill *Loxia curvirostra*
Red-eyed vireo *Vireo olivaceus*
Red-tailed hawk *Buteo jamaicensis*

Red-winged blackbird *Agelaius phoeniceus*
Ring-billed gull *Larus delawarensis*
Ring-necked duck *Aythya colaris*
Ring-necked pheasant *Phasianus colchicus*
Rock dove *Columba livia*
Rough-legged hawk *Buteo lagopus*
Rough-winged swallow *Stelgidopteryx ruficollis*
Ruby-crowned kinglet *Regulus caldendula*
Ruffed grouse *Bonasa umbellus*
Rufous hummingbird *Selasphorus rufus*
Rufous-sided towhee *Pipilo erythrophthalmus*
Sandhill crane *Grus canadensis*
Savannah sparrow *Passerculus sandwichensis*
Saw-whet owl *Aegolius acadicus*
Say's phoebe *Sayornis saya*
Screech owl *Otus asio*
Sharp-shinned hawk *Accipiter striatus*
Shoveler *Anas clypeata*
Snow goose *Chen caerulescens*
Snowy owl *Nyctea scandiaca*
Solitary sandpiper *Tringa solitaria*
Solitary vireo *Vireo solitarius*
Song sparrow *Melospiza melodia*
Sparrow hawk *Falco sparverius*
Spotted owl *Strix occidentalis*
Spotted sandpiper *Actitis macularia*
Spruce grouse *Canachites canadensis*
Starling *Sturnus vulgaris*
Steller's jay *Cyanocitta stelleri*
Swainson's hawk *Buteo swainsoni*
Swainson's thrush *Hylocichla ustulata*
Townsend's solitaire *Myadestes townsendi*
Townsend's warbler *Dendroica townsendi*

Traill's flycatcher *Empidonax traillii*
Tree sparrow *Spizella arborea*
Tree swallow *Iridoprocne bicolor*
Turkey *Meleagris gallopavo*
Turkey vulture *Cathartes aura*
Varied thrush *Ixoreus naevius*
Vaux's swift *Chaetura vauxi*
Vesper sparrow *Pooecetes gramineus*
Violet-green swallow *Tachycineta thalassina*
Virginia rail *Rallus limicola*
Warbling vireo *Vireo gilvus*
Water pipit *Anthus spinoletta*
Western bluebird *Sialia mexicana*
Western flycatcher *Empidonax difficilis*
Western grebe *Aechmophorus occidentalis*
Western kingbird *Tyrannus verticalis*
Western meadowlark *Sturnella neglecta*
Western tangager *Piranga ludoviciana*
Western wood peewee *Contopus sordidulus*
Whistling swan *Olor columbianus*
White-crowned sparrow *Zonotrichia leucophrys*
White-fronted goose *Anser albifrons*
White-headed woodpecker *Picoides albolarvatus*
White-tailed ptarmigan *Lagopus leucurus*
Williamson's sapsucker *Sphyrapicus thyroideus*
Wilson's warbler *Wilsonia pusilla*
Winter wren *Troglodytes troglodytes*
Wood duck *Aix sponsa*
Yellow-bellied sapsucker *Sphyrapicus varius*
Yellow-breasted chat *Icteria virens*
Yellowthroat *Geothlypis trichas*
Yellow warbler *Dendroica petechia*

Reptiles

Common garter snake *Thamnophis sirtalis*

Ensatina *Ensatina eschscholtzi*

Long-toed salamander *Ambystoma macrodactylum*

Northern alligator lizard *Gerrhonotus coeruleus*

Northwestern garter snake *Thamnophis ordinoides*

Northwestern salamander *Ambystoma gracile*

Pacific giant salamander *Dicamptodon ensatus*

Pine gopher snake *Pituophis melanoleucus*

Racer *Coluber constrictor*

Rubber boa *Charina bottae*

Van Dyke's salamander *Plethodon vandykei*

Western fence lizard *Sceloporus occidentalis*

Western terrestrial garter snake *Thamnophis elegans*

Western red-backed salamander *Plethodon vehiculum*

Western skink *Eumeces skiltonianus*

Amphibians

Bullfrog *Rana catesbeiana*

Cascades frog *Rana cascadae*

Leopard frog *Rana pipiens*

Northern rough-skinned newt *Taricha granulosa granulosa*

Pacific tree frog *Hyla regilla*

Red-legged frog *Rana aurora*

Tailed frog *Ascaphus truei*

Western toad *Bufo boreus*

Fish

American shad *Alosa sapidissima*

Black crappie *Pomoxis nigromaculatus*

Bluegill *Lepomis macrochirus*

Brook trout *Salvelinus fontinalis*

Brown bullhead *Ictalurus nebulosus*

Carp *Cyprinus carpio*

Chinook (King salmon) *Oncorhynchus tshawytscha*

Chiselmouth *Acrocheilus alutaceus*

Coastal cutthroat trout *Salmo clarkii clarkii*

Coastrange sculpin *Cottus aleuticus*

Coho (Silver salmon) *Oncorhynchus kisutch*

Dolly Varden *Salvelinus malma*

Largemouth bass *Micropterus salmoides*

Large-scale sucker *Catostomus macrocheilus*

Long-nosed dace *Rhinichthys cataractae*

Mountain sucker *Catostomus platyrhynchus*

Mountain whitefish *Prosopium williamsoni*

Northern squawfish *Ptychocheilus oregonensis*

Pacific lamprey *Entosphenus tridentatus*

Peamouth *Mylocheilus caurinus*

Piute sculpin *Cottus beldingi*

Rainbow trout (Steelhead) *Salmo gairdneri*

Redside shiner *Richardsonius balteatus*

Reticulate sculpin *Cottus perplexus*

River lamprey *Lampetra ayresi*

Sand roller *Percopsis transmontana*

Shorthead sculpin *Cottus confusus*

Sockeye salmon (Kokanee) *Oncorhynchus nerka*

Speckled dace *Rhinichthys osculus*

Western brook lamprey *Lampetra richardsoni*

White sturgeon *Acipenser transmontanus*

Yellow perch *Perca flavescens*

Bibliography

Suggested Reading

Bullard, F. M. 1976. *Volcanoes of the Earth*. University of Texas Press, Austin. 579 p.

Crandell, D. R., and Mullineaux, D. R. 1978. *Potential Hazards from Future Eruptions of Mount St. Helens Volcano*. U.S. Geological Survey, Washington, D.C. Bulletin 1383-C. 26 p.

Decker, R., and Decker, B. 1981. *Volcanoes*. W. H. Freeman and Company, San Francisco. 244 p.

Foxworthy, B. L., and Hill, M. 1982. *Volcanic Eruptions of 1980 at Mount St. Helens: The First 100 Days*. U.S. Geological Survey, Washington, D.C. Professional Paper 1249. 125 p.

Francis, P. 1976. *Volcanoes*. Penguin Books, New York. 368 p.

Harris, S. L. 1980. *Fire and Ice: The Cascade Volcanoes*. Mountaineers-Pacific Search Press, Seattle. 316 p.

Johansen, D. O., and Gates, C. M. 1967. *Empire of the Columbia*. 2nd ed. Harper and Row, New York. 654 p.

Kozloff, E. N. 1976. *Plants and Animals of the Pacific Northwest: An Illustrated Guide to the Natural History of Western Oregon, Washington, and British Columbia*. University of Washington Press, Seattle. 264 p.

Lipman, P. W., and Mullineaux, D. R., eds. 1981. *The 1980 Eruptions of Mount St. Helens*. U.S. Geological Survey, Washington, D.C. Professional Paper 1250. 844 p.

MacDonald, G. A. 1972. *Volcanoes*. Prentice-Hall, Englewood Cliffs, N.J. 510 p.

McKee, B. 1972. *Cascadia: The Geologic Evolution of the Pacific Northwest*. McGraw-Hill, New York. 394 p.

Meinig, D. W. 1968. *The Great Columbia Plain: A Historical Geography 1805–1910*. University of Washington Press, Seattle. 598 p.

Ollier, C. 1969. *Volcanoes*. The MIT Press, Cambridge. 177 p.

Williams, H., and McBirney, A. R. 1979. *Volcanology*. Freeman, Cooper and Company, San Francisco. 397 p.

References Cited

Brugman, M. M., and Meier, M. F. 1981. "Response of Glaciers to the Eruptions of Mount St. Helens." In P. W. Lipman and D. R. Mullineaux, eds., *The 1980 Eruptions of Mount St. Helens,* pp. 743–56. U.S. Geological Survey, Washington, D.C. Professional Paper 1250.

Burke, G. 1959. "Indian Zack's Alarm Saved the Lewis River Settlers." *Cowlitz County Historical Quarterly,* 1(2):8–9.

Burnett, P. H. 1902. "Letters of Peter H. Burnett." *Oregon Historical Quarterly,* 3:423–24.

Cox A., ed. 1973. *Plate Tectonics and Geomagnetic Reversals.* W. H. Freeman and Company, San Francisco. 702 p.

Deitz, R. S., and Holden, J. C. 1970. "The Breakup of Panaea." *Scientific American,* 223(4):30–41.

Dewey, J. F. 1972. "Plate Tectonics." In J. T. Wilson, ed. 1976. *Continents Adrift and Continents Aground: Readings from Scientific American,* pp. 34–45. W. H. Freeman and Company, San Francisco.

Dion, N. P., and Embrey, S. S. 1981. *Effects of Mount St. Helens Eruption on Selected Lakes in Washington.* U.S. Geological Survey, Washington, D.C. Circular 850-G. 25 p.

Fugro Northwest, Inc. 1980. *Cultural Resource Assessment for the Cowlitz Falls Hydroelectric Project,* pp. 8–15. R. W. Beck and Associates, Seattle.

Irwin, J. 1979. "The Cowlitz Way: A Round of Life." *Cowlitz County Historical Quarterly,* 21(1):5–24.

Jermann, J. V., and Mason, R. D. 1976. *A Cultural Resource Overview of the Gifford Pinchot National Forest, South-Central Washington.* University of Washington Office of Public Archaeology, Institute for Environmental Studies, Seattle. 217 p.

Kane, P. 1971. "Wanderings of an Artist Among the Indians of North America." In J. R. Harper, ed., *Paul Kane's Frontier,* pp. 97–98. Amon Carter Museum, Fort Worth. Reprint of the 1859 edition.

Lewis, M., and Clark, W. 1905. *Original Journals of the Lewis and Clark Expedition, 1804–1806.* 8 vols. Ed. R. G. Thwaites. 3:195–96. 4:220. Dodd, Mead and Company, New York.

Loo-Wit Lat-Kla. 1861. *Gold Hunting in the Cascade Mountains.* Printed at the Chronicle Office by L.E.V. Coon. 27 p.

Macmahon, J. A. 1982. "Mount St. Helens Revisited." *Natural History,* 91(5):14–24.

Majors, H. H. 1980. "Mount St. Helens Series." *Northwest Discovery,* 1(1):1–51, 2:68–108.

Parrish, J. L. 1906. "Letter Dated January 13, 1892 to W. G. Steel." *Steel Points,* 1(1):25–26.

Ray, V. F. 1966. *Handbook of Cowlitz Indians.* Northwest Copy Company, Seattle. 44 p.

Sarna-Wojciciki, A. M., S. Shipley, R. B. Waitt, Jr., D. Dzurisin, and S. H. Wood. 1981. "Areal Distribution, Thickness, Mass, Volume, and Grain Size of Air-Fall from the Six Major Eruptions of Mount St. Helens, Washington." In P. W. Lipman and D. R. Mullineaux, eds., *The 1980 Eruptions of Mount St. Helens,* pp. 577–600. U.S. Geological Survey, Washington, D.C. Professional Paper 1250.

Spurr, S. H., and Barnes, B. V. 1980. *Forest Ecology.* John Wiley and Sons, New York. 687 p.

Swanson, D. A., T. J. Casadevall, and D. Dzurisin. 1983. "Predicting Eruptions at Mount St. Helens: June 1980 Through December 1982." *Science,* 221(4618):1369–75.

Tilling, R. I. 1982. *Volcanoes.* U.S. Geological Survey. "Popular Publications of the U.S. Geological Survey." 44 p.

Tolmie, W. F. 1963. *The Journals of William Fraser Tolmie: Physician and Fur Trader.* Mitchell Press Limited, Vancouver, B.C. 181 p.

Toksoz, M. N. 1975. "The Subduction of the Lithosphere." *Scientific American, 223(5):88–98.*

USDA, Forest Service. 1984. "Mount St. Helens National Volcanic Monument: Draft Environmental Impact Statement, Comprehensive Management Plan." Pacific Northwest Region, Portland, Oregon. 326 p.

Vancouver, G. 1968. *A Voyage of Discovery to the North Pacific Ocean and the World.* Da Capo Press, New York. 1:259, 421–22. Reprint of the original London 1798 edition.

Wilkes, C. et al. 1845. *Narrative of the United States Exploring Expedition: During the Years 1838, 1839, 1840, 1841, 1842.* 4:439–40. Lea and Blanchard, Philadelphia.

Yamaguchi, D. K. 1983. "New Tree-Ring Dates for Recent Eruptions of Mount St. Helens." Quaternary Research 20, pp. 246–50. University of Washington, Seattle.

Index

Numbers in **boldface** refer to photographs, graphs, or diagrams

162

Credits

(Photographs not listed were taken by the author.)

Photographs

A. B. Adams: p. 34
A. B. Adams and Virginia Dale, 35
Richard Barden: p. 89
A. J. Irving: pp. 46, 53, 54
E. Merrill: p. 33
National Park Service: p. 73
Keith Ronnholm: pp. 2, 10, 110-11
Royal Ontario Museum: p. 78
Rick Sugg: p. 45
U.S. Forest Service: pp. 13, 62, 65, 66, 67, 74, 75, 76, 84, 85; Roland Emetay: p. 132; Jim Hughes: pp. 4, 12, 18, 36, 133; Wayne Parsons: p. 21; Barbara Taubman: p. 22; F. Valenzuela: p. 30
U.S. Geological Survey: pp. 9, 26; Harry Glicken: p. 7; Terry Leighley: p. 14; Dee Molenaar: p. 6; Austin Post: p. 5; Lyn Topinka: pp. 8, 17, 24, 57, 94

Diagrams, Charts, and Maps

Page

16-17: Ted Reeves, *The Oregonian*
20: Yamaguchi 1983
43: Ollier 1976; Bullard 1976
48: Foxworthy and Hill 1982; Decker and Decker 1981; Tilling 1982
49: Dewey 1972; Tilling 1982
55: Foxworthy and Hill 1982; Harris 1980
64: Fugro Northwest, Inc., 1980
88: Brugman and Meier 1981

Scott Shane *completed his graduate studies in forestry at the University of Washington with Mount St. Helens as his thesis topic. He worked at Mount St. Helens National Volcanic Monument for two seasons as a naturalist and was the first person to lead the public into the devastated zone and provide interpretive discussion. He and his wife Rebecca Andrews-Shane are avid mountaineers who have hiked throughout the Cascade Range.*